Social Work and

Child and Adolescent
Mental Health

Steven Walker

Russell House Publishing

First published in 2003 by:
Russell House Publishing Ltd.
4 St George's House
Uplyme Road
Lyme Regis
Dorset DT7 3LS

Tel: 01297-443948
Fax: 01297-442722
e-mail: help@russellhouse.co.uk
www.russellhouse.co.uk

British Library Cataloguing-in-publication Data:
A catalogue record for this book is available from the British Library.

ISBN: 1-903855-22-5

Typeset by TW Typesetting, Plymouth, Devon.

Printed by Antony Rowe, Chippenham, Wiltshire

About Russell House Publishing

RHP is a group of social work, probation, education and
youth and community work practitioners and academics
working in collaboration with a professional publishing
team.
Our aim is to work closely with the field to produce
innovative and valuable materials to help managers,
trainers, practitioners and students.
We are keen to receive feedback on publications and
new ideas for future projects.

Contents

To Isobel and Rose

Acknowledgements

This book has one author but many contributors. Some are explicitly referenced while others have not published but their ideas have affected me in ways that are just as important. They are the children and adolescents with whom I have worked and the colleagues in social work and elsewhere who have influenced my professional development. It is almost impossible to record all of the people who have in a small or larger way helped me reach a position where I can write on such an important subject. Their absence from this acknowledgement does not reflect the size of their particular contribution, rather the limits of my memory and available space. Staff at the London School of Economics, Maudsley Hospital, Tavistock Institute and the Institiute of Family Therapy were all especially helpful in the development of my interest in child and adolescent mental health, social work and family therapy qualifications. Shula Ramon, Rose Rackman, Eric Taylor, Barry Mason, Damian McCann, and David Campbell were especially influential. I want to thank Jane Dutton and Annie Turner who were two of the most intelligent and supportive managers any member of staff could wish for when I was in practice. In my academic role I owe a big debt to Kate Atherton and Leslie Dobree for providing me with the opportunity to develop my research and teaching interests and for the sabbatical time to complete this manuscript. Diane DeBell and Charlie Davison both contributed enormously to the improvement of my research skills. Steve Herington, Anna Perera, Andrew Maynard and Andy Whittaker all provided thoughtful and constructive feedback on early drafts of the book. I am particularly indebted to Geoffrey Mann and Martin Calder at Russell House Publishing for encouraging me in this project and for their kindness and professionalism throughout the process from proposal to publication. On a more personal note, writing a book about child and adolescent mental health and drawing on all the influences on my thinking about the subject necessarily means reflecting on my own childhood. Fortunately the ground was prepared in the years I spent in therapy with Nina Farhi soon after embarking on my career in social work. That work cannot possibly be quantified and the depth of my debt to her cannot be adequately measured. Neither can the love and support of my wife Isobel and daughter Rose who have had to endure my physical and temporal absence in the long hours of text production, as well as the unglamorous side effects of fatigue, frustration and determination to complete the book. They are my foundation and deserve the biggest thank you of all for the unconditional love, care and faith that helped sustain me and really made this book possible.

Foreword

The role of social work in a comprehensive child and adolescent mental health service (CAMHS) has changed indecisively in recent years. As child and family social work has focused more on protection and less on prevention and early intervention, the social work task has not been about children's mental health. Many social services departments have felt the specialist CAMHS are too remote from the core task and often not appreciating CAMHS input and role have withdrawn from the specialist multi-disciplinary teams.

There has been some re-engagement with the introduction in 1998 of the CAMHS grant to finance service improvement. Joint strategies have emerged and progress has been made in developing mental health services in partnership, particularly with the Quality Protects agenda. The concept of the comprehensive CAMHS – set out in the thematic review 'Together We Stand' – is now more generally understood, and the significant role of the social worker in relation to the mental health of the child is more fully appreciated.

This book is therefore timely. It addresses, thoughtfully and comprehensively, the input that the social worker needs to make to support the mental health of vulnerable children and young people. The basic social work training does not provide enough to support people coming into the profession to do that most crucial and skilled task. This book is a significant contribution towards ensuring that the troubled and troubling young people, for whom social workers are given responsibility, are strong enough in their minds to manage the difficulties of their lives. This resilience, this precious and inadequately understood quality, is something a skilled social worker can promote and support in a child.

This book is located at the heart of how a modern social work practice should be. It embraces a wide theoretical panorama rooted in social justice, evidence-based practice, and the psycho-social core of social work. To borrow the author's words, 'social workers' special contribution to CAMHS work is in their unique capacity to hold onto the external reality while maintaining the capacity to stay with the pain of each family's situation.' This is a powerful position. This book helps social workers to use it effectively, collaborating with others in the field, employing appropriate techniques, and in so doing, ensuring that the mental health of the most vulnerable of our children is developed and safeguarded.

Dinah Morley
Deputy Director, Young Minds

Introduction

Grown-ups never understand anything for themselves, and it is tiresome for children to be always and forever explaining things to them.
(Saint-Exupery, 1943).

Evidence of the rising numbers and specific characteristics of child and adolescent mental health problems has been thoroughly documented, prompting widespread professional, public and private concern (ONS, 2001; Dimigen et al., 1999; Mental Health Foundation, 1999; Kurtz, 1996; Rutter and Smith, 1995; Rutter, 1995). Social workers are at the heart of this phenomenon working in the front line where children, families, parent/carers, schools and communities are experiencing the destructive consequences.

The traditional model of service delivery in community child and adolescent mental health care in Britain began to emerge after the child guidance council was set up in 1928 to 'encourage the provision of skilled treatment of children showing behaviour disturbances and early symptoms of disorder'. This was the result of pressure from Education and Health officials, who were concerned about the abilities and behavioural problems of children brought into the new state compulsory education system at the beginning of the 20th century. These developments were also influenced by innovations in the USA, where the first child guidance clinic was established in a deprived neighbourhood in 1909 in Chicago.

The interplay between social deprivation and children's emotional problems had begun to be correlated-highlighting the need for a social work dimension to assessment and intervention in this area that has endured to this day (Crutcher, 1943). The service was comprised of a multidisciplinary team of various professionals with Health, Education, and Social Work backgrounds who all brought their separate training, theoretical models, and working practices under one clinical umbrella. Over the next fifty years child guidance clinics grew in number and became accessible to more and more children and families.

Their aims were to intervene with children and families referred for help in a variety of ways where there were concerns about a child's mental health, behaviour, or emotional development. Each team member had distinctive skills and worked with the child, parents, or whole family. Traditionally the psychiatrist would lead the team and be responsible for clinical diagnosis. Social workers would support parents. Psychotherapists worked with children individually, while education staff focused on learning ability and liaison with teachers.

However, their success in offering support to parents resulted in increasing demand, the creation of long waiting lists, delays in treatment, and pressure to prioritise the most urgent and worrying cases. These would invariably include children with severe and longstanding mental health problems, aggressive or disturbed behaviour, school learning problems, physical, sexual or emotional abuse, depression, acute anxiety, and suicidal behaviour.

The need to develop child and adolescent mental health services (CAMHS) has attracted more attention in recent years due to increased demands on specialist resources by parents, teachers, social workers, and primary health care staff. Attempting to meet the needs of children suffering emotional and behavioural problems as well as their carers and families, has proved onerous. The evidence has suggested the need for policy and practice changes to ensure a sufficient range of provision and skills to improve the effectiveness and efficiency of CAMHS (Goodman, 1997; DoH, 1997; Audit Commission, 1999; Mental Health Foundation, 1999; Walker, 2001a).

Recent studies from several different countries agree fairly closely that the prevalence of mental health problems in children up to the age of 18 years is 10 per cent, with higher rates among groups that suffer a number of risk factors such as those who live in many poor, inner city environments (Audit Commission, 1998). It is estimated that in Britain, one in five children and young people manifest mild emotional or behavioural difficulties or the early stage of significant problems that do not require long-term specialist intervention. However, only a small proportion of these children actually present to services for help, manifesting difficulties in a variety of contexts where the cause of the problem is not adequately addressed. Many social work staff lack confidence in assessing and intervening even when they suspect a mental health component to the difficulties being presented (Mental Health Foundation, 1999).

This book aims to provide a resource for social workers in a variety of contexts in voluntary or statutory agencies who may encounter situations where concerns are expressed about the behaviour, emotional state, or mental health of a child or young person. This could be in child protection, young offenders, family support, long term planning, fostering and adoption, juvenile justice, education social work, probation, and of course child and adolescent mental health services. The book aspires to provide a foundation of theoretical ideas and practical guidance that will offer support and create the basis for informed, reflective, confident practice.

I have not sought to define social work *per se* as that task has been more than adequately addressed over the years in several excellent texts where the plethora of definitions and debates about 'what is social work' can be examined in detail. Rather I take the view that there is a consensus among both seasoned professionals and newly qualified practitioners that social work is at its most helpful when practice starts from the understanding that people exist in a social context with their own deeply personal psychological strengths and vulnerabilities. Competent social work therefore is able to bear both these dimensions in mind, and the interaction between them when assessing and intervening.

   Social work in the field of child and adolescent mental health is an awesome undertaking. It covers the majority of the most intense and rapidly changing periods of human growth and development, within which are laid the foundations for much of what will transpire in the rest of a person's life. The social work contribution is therefore crucial bringing as it does a social dimension to a child or young person's emotional and behavioural experience at a time when effective intervention can make a difference for the present and in the future. I have sought to provide social workers a varied menu to choose from of accessible and useful resources and information gleaned from contemporary sources of evidence-based literature and quality research, as well as from my own experience in CAMHS work. These are designed to be applied in whatever context social workers practice, from primary through to specialist levels of support in voluntary or statutory agencies.

   This book examines an area of social work practice that has rarely been encapsulated in one volume. It covers the wider policy and legal context of child and adolescent mental health problems and how services for this group of young people are organised and delivered. Definitions and prevalence of various mental health problems are elucidated and underpinned by contemporary quantitative data concerning signs, symptoms and resilience factors. Practice guidance will illuminate the crucial area of social work assessment and the different contexts in which children and adolescents become vulnerable to developing mental health problems.

   Culturally competent practice is described and discussed in order to distinguish the particular needs of a diverse multi-cultural and ethnically rich society. Methods and models of social work intervention, and their underpinning theories are systematically organised to offer a broad repertoire of helping strategies to aid practitioner skill development. The importance of multi-disciplinary and inter-professional care is explored to help social workers locate their practice within the appropriate network of statutory and voluntary resources to fulfil the aim of holistic support.

   The concept of social inclusion receives full attention. How this critical area of governmental policy impacts and offers opportunities in this area of social work practice is analysed and reviewed. Partnership practice and service user evaluation is a growing area of interest in social work practice. This concept is developed and applied to the area of child and adolescent mental health in the final chapter to illustrate the potential of an empowering, child-focused design and delivery of services that meets the needs and responds to the agenda of young people themselves. Finally, a selected list of organisations that can offer resources directly or indirectly in child and adolescent mental health that are accessible to children and young people themselves or for parents and practitioners has been included.

   The world of the child or young person suffering mental health problems is a lonely, isolated one. Often it is a silent agony that corrodes the sense of self and produces wretched feelings, fear, dismay and hopelessness. When these troubles surface and become noticed by peers, parents or professionals their responses are too often punitive, blaming or inconsiderate. Adults can also feel helpless, confused and frightened by the manifestation of mental health problems in children. This book tries to reduce the gap between children and young people and others concerned about their mental health. It offers social workers in this most quintessential area of practice, ways of helping, supporting and managing the internal and external resources necessary to respond appropriately.

Terminology

The term children and young person is used throughout this text generally to include people up to the age of 18 years. Specific reference to infants will be used to describe work with children up to five years; school age children up to 12 years; and adolescents up to 18 years of age. These are of course arbitrary distinctions covering a wide variety of developmental and cognitive differences, but they will hopefully help the reader navigate to areas of specific interest whilst avoiding unnecessary repetition or confusion. The term parent/carers is used to highlight the important role played by non-biological adults in the upbringing of children and young people.

Family is a term used in its broadest sense to incorporate diverse forms of social groupings that do not necessarily fit the nuclear, heterosexual normative model. Black is used in the text to include every ethnic group subjected to institutional and personal racism that results in the devaluing of ethnic minority culture. The term mental health problems is used generically to cover psychiatric terminology that is not appropriate for the intended readership and to avoid unnecessary repetition of the variety and severity of different emotional and behavioural difficulties faced by children and young people.

CHAPTER 1

The Policy and Legislative Context

Introduction

There is a long history in the social science literature of interest and concern by welfare policy makers in the emotional and psychological health of the country's citizens influenced by studies of family life (Kay-Shuttleworth, 1832; Comte, 1852; Murdock, 1949; Young and Wilmott, 1957). This lineage can be traced to contemporary evidence providing a developing picture of changing family characteristics which have accelerated over the past twenty five years across Europe and North America (Utting, 1995; McGlone et al., 1998; NCH Action for Children, 2000; Bradshaw, 2001). Governments and health and social work professionals' attempts to intervene to support family life have been criticised for too much or too little interference. However, there is an increasing consensus that the emotional and behavioural life of children and young people requires more support and understanding than ever before. The increased volume, complexity, and severity of contemporary child and adolescent mental health problems has attracted much more recent concern and intensified efforts to respond (Webster-Stratton, 1997; Gordon and Grant, 1997; Carr, 2000; Clarke, 2001).

Attempts to understand the causes of this relatively recent historical phenomenon can be located in social policy discourse across the spectrum of political philosophy. The patrician right cite the breakdown of traditional values and lack of respect for authority, the liberal/left blame the socially divisive consequences of unbridled *laissez faire* capitalism, while the libertarian right argue that the nanny state and meddlesome welfare professionals are hindering individual choice to a free lifestyle, thereby causing stress. All of these positions are trying to understand the same problem and using the same sources of evidence to justify their conclusions. Whatever conclusions are drawn, there seems little doubt that the evidence of changes in family life, the effects on the mental health of children and adolescents, and their modern environmental context are linked.

The number of divorces, the increase in single parent households, and increased cohabitation, has contributed to a sense of structural change in the pattern of contemporary family relationships. The widening gap between rich and poor highlight the needs of those families socially excluded, marginalised and disempowered. There are increased numbers of mothers in work; the ageing of the population is causing concern about demographic imbalance. Drug and alcohol abuse and the rise in youth homelessness contribute to a sense of disaffection and alienation in young people. These external factors are interacting with intra-familial stressors such as the increased reporting of domestic violence, child abuse, and the rise in teenage pregnancy, which are all cited as evidence of the consequences of the pressures and strains put on modern family life. Racism and xenophobia have also increased as European Union enlargement has accelerated population migration. Armed conflict has precipitated increased numbers of asylum seekers with economic and social dislocation prompting more refugee applications to wealthier member countries (Walker, 2002).

These changes in the socio-geographic texture of Europe have produced moral panics and hasty policy changes to tackle the phenomena described, or at least they have forced governments to address the symptoms consistent with such rapid sociological change. However, services for children and families attempting to prevent some of the negative consequences of such changes, have traditionally been low priorities. Services for adult mental health have always been a low priority despite the evidence of the link with disturbance in children of parents with mental health problems. Services for child mental health have been even more neglected, under-funded and have further suffered because of the confusion and ambiguities about how they should be delivered and by whom.

Social workers are positioned at the interface between the economic, social and psychological and therefore ideally placed to work with children and young people suffering with or at risk of developing mental health problems. This can include offering practical support to parents/carers, advocacy for services to regenerate communities, and interpersonal skills to strengthen the internal and external resources required to promote mental health in children and young people.

Organisational context

In 1997 the British House of Commons Health Committee fourth report on expenditure, administration, and policy, focused on child and adolescent mental health services. This took place in the context of demands from parents, and staff in Education, Health and Social Work services overwhelmed by needs they were unable to meet (House of Commons, 1997). The Committee noted the significance of mental health as one of five key areas in the Conservative government's Health of the Nation programme. It suggested that the Department of Health should adopt indicators and targets for children, including the setting of a target to reduce child suicides, and a target for the reduction of specific disorders.

Later in 1997 the new Labour government pledged itself to change the NHS internal market and lay the foundation for a new approach based on co-operation rather than competition between all stakeholders. The aim was to promote partnership as one of the key strategic commissioning objectives to deliver best outcomes for local populations from the resources available to them (DoH, 1997). Assembling the findings of three influential pieces of research and combining them with government policy statements, enabled the design of a set of guidelines for CAMH service providers as shown in Table 1.1 (Kurtz (Ed.), 1992; Kurtz et al., 1994; HAS, 1995; Audit Commission, 1998).

The need for such guidelines had been an important step towards establishing some commonality and equity in service provision. Mental health services for children and adolescents are generally poorly planned and historically determined rather than needs led. Their geographical distribution is patchy and they are variable in quality and composition. The work they do often seems unrelated in strength or diversity to assessed population need. Child and Adolescent Mental Health Services comprise the specifically trained resources in child and adolescent mental health available for a particular population. In 1995 CAMHS were found to be managed and delivered often in more than one health trust, and in more than one agency, thwarting attempts to co-ordinate care (HAS, 1995). Services for the mental health of children and adolescents aim to:

- Promote mental health in young people.
- Prevent problems occurring.
- Treat and manage problems and disorders that do arise so that their adverse impacts are minimised.

The national picture in child and adolescent mental health services is still characterised by long waiting times, and uneven distribution of specialist provision. Obscure access routes for service user pathways combine with excessive pressure on primary preventive services in health and social care, resulting in poor levels of inter-agency co-operation. The outcome is to create barriers to those most disadvantaged and socially excluded families requiring help. The government National Priorities Guidance, Modernising Health and Social Services (1998), states that one of its mental health objectives is to:

Improve provision of appropriate high quality care and treatment for children and young people by building up locally-based child and adolescent mental health services. This should be achieved through . . . improved liaison between primary care, specialist CAMHS, social services and other agencies.

This was the first time that National Priorities Guidance was directed jointly at local authorities and health authorities. Local authorities were given the lead on children's welfare and interagency working. Local authorities and health authorities were to share lead on mental health and reducing health inequalities. There is evidence of similar developments aimed at preventing mental health difficulties progressing, and responding quickly to those that occur (Nixon and Northrup, 1997).

Table 1.1: CAMHS service provider guidelines (Audit Commission, 1998)

Relationships with commissioners

- The service should be represented on a group that regularly advises commissioners and purchasers about arrangements for delivering comprehensive child and adolescent mental health services.
- The CAMHS should have a plan which reflects an understanding of how the purchasers perceive the contribution of this *specialist* service as part of the delivery of the *full* child and adolescent mental health service.

Top level trust planning

- There should be an operational policy for CAMHS.
- There should be a recognisable and separate budget for the CAMHS.
- There should be an awareness of the major elements of CAMHS expenditure.
- Services should be child-centred and responsive to age-related and other particular needs, such as those of families from minority ethnic groups.
- Services should have protocols for dealing with confidentiality.
- Services should be provided in a welcoming environment, with buildings and rooms safe and suitable for children and young people.
- There should be service level agreements to cover consultancy and advice for consultant colleagues in other specialties such as paediatrics. Agreements should ensure that the service provides regular and adequate input to children's homes, EBD schools, secure units, and to other groups of young people at particular risk.
- There should be provision for adequate specialist mental health support to social workers, teachers, GPs and others.
- The CAMHS should be provided by a multidisciplinary team or through a network. Health service personnel will make up only a part of the team – appropriate input from social services and education departments should also be maintained.
- There should be a clear relationship with adult Mental Health Services.

Operations

- There should be an adequate information system geared specifically to CAMHS.
- The service should offer a relevant range of interventions to suit different needs.
- There should be clear referral channels to CAMHS which are appropriate to the referrer.
- There should be a clear access route to day patient and in-patient services.
- There should be a clear protocol for dealing with young people who present in crisis: including those who may deliberately harm themselves. There should be access to appropriately skilled 24 hour cover by mental health specialists for the child and adolescent population.
- Waiting time for the first appointment for a non-urgent condition should be less than 13 weeks.
- The service should identify topics for audit which should be undertaken regularly.
- Appropriate training should be offered to CAMHS staff, including secretarial and reception staff.

Historically, there have been difficulties in collaboration in the area of child and adolescent mental health which undermine the strategic aim of fostering closer working. These difficulties can be explained in terms of resource constraints combined with extra demands continually being placed on all statutory agencies. Other explanations emphasise in addition, the different theoretical models underpinning working practices; the importance of personality factors; and the capacity of senior managers to create an atmosphere of co-operation at all levels of the system (Pearce, 1999).

The National Service Framework for Mental Health was introduced in 2000 to try to address inequities and bring cohesion to services for mentally ill people. However the NSF did not include children and adolescents within its remit. At the time of writing the current plan is to bring child and adolescent mental health services into the National Service Framework for Children due to be published in 2003. The national children's mental health charity Young Minds has warned that excluding CAMHS from the NSF for Mental Health was a missed opportunity (Young Minds, 2001). Including it within what will necessarily be a broad NSF for Children, will dilute or obscure the current work being undertaken to improve services for this traditionally neglected area of children's lives.

For the time being the current organisational structure of child and adolescent mental health services can be represented by Table 1.2 which illustrates the four tier progressive framework through which children and young people will be referred. Social workers, whether in statutory or voluntary organisations may be involved at any of the four tiers of intervention, but the majority will be involved at Tier 1 and Tier 2. Most children or adolescents with mental health problems will be seen at Tiers 1 and 2. All agencies should have structures in place to facilitate the referral of clients between tiers, and to maximise the contribution of CAMH specialists at each tier. The importance of multi-professional and inter agency working cannot be over-emphasised in this area of work, and Chapter 6 explores this in more detail.

Legal framework

The legal framework for child and adolescent mental health encompasses a wide spectrum of social policy including juvenile justice, mental health, education, and children and family legislation. The term 'mental illness' is not defined in law relating to children and young people. The variety of legal frameworks affecting them provide the context for work undertaken by a number of health and social care staff concerned about children and young people whose behaviour is described as disturbed or disturbing. The relevant legal and ethical issues for social workers are linked to practice principles and values embedded in a psycho-social approach. Of particular interest to social workers in the context of empowering practice are the issues of consent and confidentiality. The Children's

Table 1.2: CAMHS Tiered Framework (based on the Handbook on Child and Adolescent Mental Health, 1995).

Key Components, Professionals and Functions of Tiered Child and Adolescent Mental Health Services

Tier 1. A primary level which includes interventions by:
- GPs
- health visitors
- school nurses
- social services
- voluntary agencies
- teachers
- residential social workers
- juvenile justice workers

Child and adolescent mental health services (CAMHS) at this level are provided by non-specialists who are in a position to:
- identify mental health problems early in their development
- offer general advice – and in certain cases treatment for less severe problems
- pursue opportunities for promoting mental health and preventing mental health problems

Tier 2. A level of service provided by uni-professional group which relates to others through a network (rather than within a team).

These include:
- clinical child psychologists
- paediatricians, especially community
- educational psychologists
- child psychiatrists
- community child psychiatric nurses/nurse specialists

CAMHS professionals should be able to offer:

- training and consultation to other professionals (who might be within Tier 1)
- consultation for professionals and families
- outreach to identify severe or complex needs which require more specialist interventions but where the children or families are unwilling to use specialist services
- assessment which may trigger treatment at a different tier

Tier 3. A specialist service for the more severe, complex and persistent disorders. This is usually a multi-disciplinary team or service working in a community child mental health clinic or child psychiatry out-patient service, and including:
- child and adolescent psychiatrists
- social workers
- clinical psychologists
- community psychiatric nurses
- child psychotherapists
- occupational therapists
- art, music and drama therapists

The core CAMHS in each district should be able to offer:
- assessment and treatment of child mental health disorders
- assessment for referrals to Tier 4
- contribution to the services, consultation and training at Tiers 1 & 2
- participation in R & D projects

Table 1.2: *Continued.*

Tier 4. Access to infrequently used but essential tertiary level services such as day units, highly specialist out-patient teams, and in-patient units for older children and adolescents who are severely mentally ill or at suicidal risk. These services may need to be provided on a supra-district level as not all districts can expect to offer this level of expertise. The most specialist CAMHS may provide for more than one district or region, and	should be able to offer a range of services which might include: • adolescent in-patient units • secure forensic adolescent units • eating disorder units • specialist teams for sexual abuse • specialist teams for neuro-psychiatric problems Source: Department of Health and Department of Education. A Handbook on Child and Adolescent Mental Health, 1995

Legal Centre (1994) draw attention to a number of issues regarding the rights of children and young people who might have contact with agencies on the basis of their mental health problems:

• Lack of knowledge and implementation of legal rights for children and young people to control their own medical treatment, and a general lack of rights to self-determination.

• Discrimination against children and young people on grounds of disability, race, culture, colour, language, religion, gender, and sexuality which can lead to categorisation as mentally ill and subsequent intervention and detention.

• Unnecessary and in some cases unlawful restriction of liberty and inadequate safeguards in mental health and other legislation for children and young people.

• Inadequate assessment and corresponding lack of care, treatment and education in the criminal justice system.

• Use of drugs for containment rather than treatment purposes in the community, schools, and in other institutions, combined with a lack of knowledge of consent procedures.

• Placement of children on adult wards in psychiatric hospitals.

• Lack of clear ethical guidelines for extreme situations such as force-feedings in cases of anorexia, care of suicide risk young people, and care of HIV positive or AIDS patients.

Children with mental health problems may move between four overlapping systems: criminal justice, social services, education and the health service. Children are not always helped by the appropriate service since this often depends on the resources available in the area at the time. It also depends on

Table 1.3: Agency responses to the same presenting problem (after Malek, 1993)

Juvenile justice	Social services	Education	Psychiatry
Aggression	Aggression	Aggression	Aggression
↓	↓	↓	↓
Referral to police: decision to charge	Referral to social services	Referral to education department	Referral to child psychiatrist
↓	↓	↓	↓
Pre-sentence report completed	Social work assessment conducted	Educational psychology assessment	Psychiatric assessment
↓	↓	↓	↓
Sentenced to custody	Decision to accommodate	Placed in residential school	Admitted to regional in-patient unit
↓	↓	↓	↓
Labelled as young offender	Labelled as beyond parental control	Labelled as having learning difficulty	Labelled as mentally ill

how different professional staff may perceive the behaviour of a particular child, and the vocabulary used by the service in which they work.

A youth offending team member may talk about a young person engaged in anti-social activity, a teacher about poor concentration and aggressive behaviour, and a social worker may perceive a needy, anxious, abused child. All are describing the same child.

The pathway of a child into these systems is crucial because the consequences for subsequent intervention can either exacerbate the behaviour or help to reduce it, and Table 1.3 illustrates schematically potential agency responses to the same presenting problem. The Crime and Disorder Act 1998 and the Special Educational Needs and Disability Act 2001 provide the legislative framework for youth justice and children with special educational needs. In both cases, children and young people with mental health problems may find they are being inappropriately dealt with under these Acts. The Mental Health Act 1983, the Children Act 1989 and the Human Rights Act 1998, are currently the three significant pieces of legislation providing the context for social work practice in child and adolescent mental health.

Mental Health Act 1983

The Mental Health Act 1983 is a piece of legislation designed mainly for adults with mental health problems and amongst other things sets the framework for the assessment and potential compulsory admission of patients to hospital. The majority of children in psychiatric hospitals or units are informal patients. They do not have the same access to safeguards available to adult patients detained under the Mental Health Act 1983. Children under 16 are frequently admitted by their parents even though they may not have wanted to be admitted. This is *de facto* detention. The number of children admitted to NHS psychiatric units has risen in recent years. In 1995, 4,891 children and young people under 19 were admitted in England. By 2000 the number had raised to 5,788, an increase of 18 per cent. This is a worrying trend, which is also reflected in the adult statistics for compulsory admissions. Health and Social Care policy is meant to be shifting resources away from institutional based provision to community care, but in the context of troubled young people the reverse appears to be the case.

Parts 2 and 3 of the Mental Health Act 1983 provide for compulsory admission and continued detention where a child or young person is deemed to have, or suspected of having, a mental disorder. The mental disorder must be specified as mental illness, psychopathic disorder, learning disability, or severe mental impairment. Learning disability is not stated as such in the Act, and as with psychopathic disorder, it must be associated with abnormally aggressive or seriously irresponsible conduct. Full assessment and treatment orders under sections 2 and 3 require an application to be made by the nearest relative or a social worker approved under the Mental Health Act, together with medical recommendation by two doctors. Social workers have a role whether as ASWs or not in safeguarding the rights of children and young people at these rare and acute episodes in their lives. The sections of the Mental Health Act 1983 most likely to be used with children and young people are:

- **Section 2**: for assessment for possible admission for up to 28 days
- **Section 4**: for an emergency assessment for up to 72 hours admission
- **Section 5 (2):** for emergency detention by one doctor for up to 72 hours
- **Section 5 (4):** for emergency 6 hour detention when no doctor or social worker available
- **Section 3**: for inpatient treatment for a treatable disorder for up to 6 months

Consent

Defining the capacity of a child to make her or his own decisions and consent to intervention is not easy especially in the area of child mental health. The concept of 'Gillick competent' arose following a landmark ruling in 1985 in the House of Lords (3 All E.R. 402, 1985). That ruling held that competent children under 16 years of age can consent to and refuse advice and treatment from a doctor. Since then further court cases have modified the Gillick principle so that if either the child or any person with parental responsibility gives consent to treatment, doctors can proceed, even if one or more of these people, including the child, disagree. The concept of competent refers to a child having the capacity to understand the nature, terms and consequences of proposed treatment, or the consequences of refusing such treatment, free from pressure to comply. In practice, children are considered to be lacking in capacity to consent although this could be as a result of underestimating children's intelligence, or more likely, reflect an inability to communicate effectively with them. Courts have consistently held that children do not have sufficient understanding of death – hence the force feeding of anorexics and blood transfusions of Jehova's Witnesses.

Court of Appeal decisions have since overturned the principle that Gillick competent children can refuse treatment. Such cases involved extreme and life-threatening situations involving anorexia, blood transfusion, and severely disturbed behaviour. Importantly, the courts have indicated that any person with parental responsibility can in certain circumstances override the refusal of a Gillick competent child. This means that children under a care order or accommodated by the local authority even if considered not to have the capacity to consent, still retains the right to be consulted about proposed treatment. If a child is accommodated the social worker should always obtain the parents consent since they retain full parental responsibility (Brammer, 2003). If the child is under a care order the parents share parental responsibility with the local authority. Good practice requires the social worker in these situations to negotiate with parents about who should give consent and ensure that all views are recorded in the care plan.

Confidentiality

Children and young people require the help and advice of a wide variety of sources at times of stress and unhappiness in their lives. There are voluntary, statutory and private agencies as well as relatives or friends who they find easier to approach than parents. They may want to talk in confidence about worrying feelings or behaviour. The legal position in these circumstances is confused, with agencies and professional groups relying on voluntary codes of practice guidance. A difficult dilemma frequently arises when children are considering whether a helping service is acceptable while the staff are required to disclose information to others in certain situations for example where child protection concerns are aroused.

The agency policies should be accessible to children and clearly state the limits to confidentiality. But in doing so many practitioners know they could be discouraging the sharing of important feelings and information. Social workers know only too well the importance of establishing trust and confidence in vulnerable young people and constantly have to tread the line between facilitating sensitive communication and selecting what needs to be passed on to parents, colleagues or to third parties. Ideally, where disclosure needs to be made against a young person's wishes it is good practice to inform the young person in advance and give her or him the chance to disclose the information first.

The Data Protection Act 1984 and The Access to Personal Files Act 1987 give individuals the right to see information about them, with some limitations. Children 'of sufficient understanding' have the right of access except in certain circumstances. These are particularly relevant to social work and child mental health:

- Where disclosure would be likely to cause serious harm to the child's physical or mental health.
- Where the information would disclose the identity of another person.
- Where the information is contained within a court report.
- Where the information is restricted or prohibited from disclosure in adoption cases.
- Where the information is a statement of special education needs made under the Education Act 1981.

Children Act 1989

A child who is suffering with mental health problems may behave in ways that stretch their parents/carers capacity to cope which can result in the potential for significant harm. On the other hand a child who is being abused or neglected may come to the attention of professionals concerned initially about her/his mental health. The interactive nature of mental health and child abuse presents a considerable challenge for social workers tasked with conducting assessment work in child and family contexts. This issue is explored in more depth in Chapter 3. In terms of the Children Act social workers operate within deceptively clear guidelines. In practice however the provisions within the Act and subsequent practice guidelines have sought to bring simplicity to what are inevitably highly complex situations. The duties under the terms of the Children Act are straightforward and underpinned by the following principles:

- The welfare of the child is paramount.
- Children should be brought up and cared for within their own families wherever possible.
- Children should be safe and protected by effective interventions if at risk.
- Courts should avoid delay and only make an order if this is better than not making an order.
- Children should be kept informed about what happens to them and involved in decisions made about them.
- Parents continue to have parental responsibility for their children even when their children are no longer living with them.

The shift in emphasis heralded by the Children Act from investigative child protection to needs-led assessment for family support services is particularly significant for social workers engaged in work involving children's mental health. In harmony with a broad range of fiscal and social policy measures and neighbourhood renewal projects, it means family support is enjoying something of a renaissance and enabling social workers to practice psycho-social interventions. There is a specific legal requirement under the Act that different authorities and agencies work together to provide family support services with better liaison and a corporate approach (Brammer, 2003).

Together with the four-tier integrated child and adolescent mental health services structure, the framework is there to achieve better co-ordination and effectiveness of services to help any family with a child who has a mental health problem. This is made clear under the terms of Section 17 of the Children Act that lays a duty on local authorities to provide services for children in need. The definition of 'in need' has three elements:

- The child is unlikely to achieve or maintain, or to have the opportunity of achieving or maintaining, a reasonable standard of health or development without the provision for the child of services by a local authority.
- The child's health or development is likely to be significantly impaired, or further impaired, without provision for the child of such services.
- The child is disabled.

The Act further defines disability to include children suffering from mental disorder of any kind. In relation to the first two parts of the definition, health or development is defined to cover physical, intellectual, emotional, social or behavioural development and physical or mental health. These concepts are open to interpretation of what is meant by a 'reasonable standard of health and development', as well as the predictive implications for children having the 'opportunity' of achieving or maintaining it. However it is reasonable to include the following groups of children within this part of the definition of in need and to argue the case for preventive support where there is a risk of children developing mental health problems (Ryan, 1999):

- Children living in poverty
- Homeless children
- Children suffering the effects of racism
- Young carers
- Delinquent children
- Children separated from their parents

Some children from these groups may be truanting from school, getting involved in criminal activities, or have behaviour problems at school or home. Agency responses will tend to address the presenting problem and present an intervention to apparently address it. Assessment of the needs of individual children and families is often cursory, deficit-oriented, and static. The new Framework for the Assessment of Children in Need (2001) offers the opportunity for social workers to conduct more positive, comprehensive assessments that permit the mental health needs of children and adolescents to be illuminated.

Section 47 of The Children Act gives the local authority a duty to investigate where they suspect a child is suffering or is likely to suffer significant harm. Guidance suggests the purpose of such an investigation is to establish facts, decide if there are grounds for concern, identify risk, and decide protective action. The problem with child and adolescent mental health problems is that this guidance assumes certainty within a time-limited assessment period. The nature of emotional and behavioural difficulties is their often hidden quality combined with the child's own reluctance to acknowledge them. The interpretation of a child or young person's emotional or behavioural state is usually decided by a child and adolescent psychiatrist who may be brought into a Section 43 child assessment order that has been sought following parental lack of co-operation. The social worker in situations like this, and in full care proceedings, has a crucial role in balancing the need to protect the child with the future consequences on them and their family of oppressive investigations and interventions.

In cases where the child's competence to consent to treatment, or capacity to express their wishes and feelings is impaired, it is likely that the Children Act 1989 should be used in preference to the Mental Health Act 1983. The Children Act does not carry the same stigma and consequences of the Mental Health Act, and it provides for a child's guardian to consider all the factors and act as an independent advocate in legal proceedings. The Children Act aimed to consolidate a number of child care reforms and provide a response to the evidence of failure in children's services that had been mounting in the 1980s (DHSS, 1985).

Professional social work practice was, prior to the Children Act 1989, perceived as intrusive, legalistic and biased towards child protection investigation. The new Act tried to redress the balance towards identifying needs and providing support to parents to prevent harm or neglect of children and young people. Contemporary debate about the Children Act is still concerned with how to translate the widely endorsed principles of the legislation into practical help for child welfare service users and providers (O'Hagan, 1996). In the context of child and adolescent mental health this requires social workers to optimise professional knowledge, skills, and values in a very complex area of practice.

One of the distinctive roles for social workers in this context is that of advocate. This may seem contradictory in cases where the local authority is acting in the child's best interests, but in terms of establishing trust, respect, and relationship building, supporting a complaint has benefit. Section 26 of the Children Act provides for a complaints procedure through which children and young people can appeal against decisions reached by social workers. There are informal and formal stages to the procedure with an expectation that an independent person is included at the formal stages. When these procedures have been exhausted a judicial review can be applied for within 3 months of the decision being appealed against. The three grounds for succeeding with judicial review are:

- Ultra vires: the social services department did not have the power to make the decision.
- Unfair: the decision was reached in a procedurally unfair manner, or by abuse of power.
- Unreasonable: all relevant matters were not considered, the law was not properly applied, or there was insufficient consultation.

Human Rights Act 1998

The Human Rights Act (UN, 1998) came into force in 2000 and incorporates into English law most of the provisions of the European Convention on Human Rights. The Act applies to all authorities undertaking functions of a public nature, including all care providers in the public sector. The Human Rights Act supports the protection and improvement of the health and welfare of children and young people throughout the United Kingdom. **Article 3** concerns freedom from torture and inhuman or degrading treatment. Children and young people who have been subjected to restraint, seclusion, or detention as a result of alarming behaviour could use this part of the Act to raise complaints.

   Article 5 concerns the right to liberty, and together with **Article 6** concerning the right to a fair hearing, are important to children and young people detained under a section of the Mental Health Act, the Children Act, or within the youth justice system. Social workers involved in such work must ensure that detention is based on sound opinion, in accordance with clearly laid out legal procedure accessible to the individual, and only lasts for as long as the mental health problem persists. In the context of youth justice work, particular attention needs to be paid to the quality and tone of pre-sentence reports which can be stigmatising. The formulaic structure of pre-sentence reports might not enable an assessing social worker working under deadline pressure, to provide an accurate picture of a young person.

   Article 8 guarantees the right to privacy and family life. Refugees and asylum seeking families can become entangled in complex legal procedures relating to citizenship and entitlement. This provision can be invoked when UK authorities are considering whether a person should be deported or remain in this country. Compassionate grounds can be used for children affected by the proposed deportation of a parent or in cases where a parent is not admitted. Social workers attuned to the attachment relationships of often small children can use this knowledge to support **Article 8** proceedings. In such circumstances the maintenance of the family unit is paramount.

Social workers involved in care proceedings or adoption work will have to consider very carefully whether such plans are in the best interests of the child but also are consistent with the child's rights under the Convention. For example, the Convention emphasises that care orders should be a temporary measure and that children should be reunited with their family as soon as possible, where appropriate. In the case of a parent with a mental health problem detained in a psychiatric hospital, the Convention could be employed by their children to facilitate regular visits if these have been denied.

Article 10 concerns basic rights to freedom of expression and in the context of children's mental health, is a crucial safeguard to ensuring that practitioners work actively to enable children and young people to express their opinions about service provision. Social workers have an opportunity within this specific provision to articulate and put into practice their value principles of partnership and children's rights.

Article 14 states that all children have an equal claim to the rights set out in the Convention 'irrespective of the child's or his or her parent's or legal guardian's race, colour, sex, language, religion, political or other opinion, national, ethnic or social origin, property, disability, birth or other status.' This provision could be used to argue for equality of service provision and non-prejudicial diagnosis or treatment. Social workers need to ensure they are employing anti-racist and non-discriminatory practice as well as facilitating children and young people to:

- Access information about their rights.
- Contact mental health services.
- Access advocates and children's rights organisations.
- Create children's service user groups.

The social work role

Social workers in a variety of work contexts in statutory or voluntary agencies, organised generically or in specialist teams, wherever they are likely to encounter children and young people as clients or carers, are potentially going to need to develop awareness and skills in child and adolescent mental health practice. In terms of the policy and organisational context advice from the Children's Legal Centre (1994) is that social workers need to follow these principles when planning to intervene in the lives of children and young people on the grounds of disturbed or disturbing behaviour:

- Fully informing the child, consulting the child and taking their views and wishes into consideration.
- Accepting that in the absence of any specific statutory limitation, children gain the right to make decisions for themselves when they have 'sufficient understanding and intelligence'.

- Respecting in particular the child's independent right to consent or withhold consent to treatment as appropriate; and where a child is incapable of giving an informed consent ensuring that the parents' consent is sought, save in emergencies.
- Ensuring that any intervention is the least restrictive alternative, and leads to the least possible segregation from the child's family, friends, community, and ordinary school.
- Children without the support of family or friends in treatment decisions should have access to independent visitors, advice, and advocacy organisations.
- In the event of a parent wishing to override the child's refusal to be treated, a legal challenge may be justified if there is evidence that the parent is not acting in the best interests of the child.

A great deal of social work will however involve delivering or commissioning family support work linked to formal or informal assessment procedures designed to find out the best way of intervening to prevent children being removed from the care of their parents or deprived of their liberty. The signs and symptoms of mental health problems may not manifest clearly, or even if they do, alternative and sometimes punitive explanations for a young person's behaviour may obscure an underlying psychological problem. Details of social work assessment and intervention strategies are provided in Chapters 3 and 5 but for now it is important to locate the social work role in this area of practice in its wider policy and professional context.

A useful way of doing this is to consider in general terms what the role of social work is in relation to other professionals working with children and families. What is it that makes social work unique and is not or rarely done by other agency staff? The first key difference is the statutory power enshrined in local authority practice contexts which always distinguishes the social work contribution to multi-agency working. The inherent capacity for compulsory sanction inevitably influences the nature of social work and affects the relationship with the service user. The second key difference is probably the training in wider social science and social policy perspectives which permits an understanding of oppressive and discriminatory processes in society. The third key difference is the explicit acknowledgement that community-focused interventions are a valuable means of empowering individuals and wider interest groups.

Together, these three elements can inform social work practice with children and adolescents who have, or are at risk of, developing mental health problems. A social model of mental health that encompasses these elements can help social workers challenge medical, institutional and punitive responses to distressed children. The social policy imperative for closer inter-professional working and reducing the barriers between staff in different agencies offers an opportunity to restate the core elements of effective social work practice. The next chapter examines how child mental health is defined and how social workers can contribute to ensure that a humanistic and holistic model for understanding the world of troubled children can be constructed.

Summary of key points

The overwhelming consensus is that over the past twenty five years there has been a detectable, statistically significant increase in the rate, volume and complexity of child and adolescent mental health problems across Europe and North America. This has caused governments, health and social care agencies, and families to seek responses and to design sustainable policies to meet the increasing demand for services.

The national picture in CAMHS is characterised by long waiting times for specialist help, patchy distribution of resources, and variable quality and composition. Inter-agency co-operation is poor with a history of different theoretical models of practice, and structural barriers to improved collaboration. The four-tier organisational structure together with national service framework guidance should improve practice.

The legal framework for CAMHS encompasses juvenile justice, human rights, mental health, education, and social services law. The issues of client consent and confidentiality are especially important in the context of children's rights principles. The interactive nature of child mental health and child abuse highlights the crucial role social workers have in understanding the legal contexts for informing assessment and intervention.

Social work principles of empowering, service-user focused practice combined with a social model of human growth and development are valuable perspectives to bring to inter-agency work in this area of practice. A psycho-social model of practice rooted in wider social science theory enables social workers to maintain an anti-discriminatory stance and value community-based solutions to child and adolescent mental health problems.

CHAPTER 2

Definitions and Prevalence

Introduction

The World Health Organisation estimates that one in five of the world's youth under 15 years of age suffer from mild to severe mental health disorders and that a large number of these children remain untreated as services to help them simply do not exist (WHO, 2001). This international context is important because within the overall figure there are significant similarities in the characteristics of problems but also differences in the prevalence rates. There is evidence to support the notion that cultural variations affect the prevalence rates, as well as figures showing consistently, for example, that boys have increased rates of externalising problems (aggression, delinquency) and that girls have increased rates of internalising problems (depression, anxiety, self-harm) (Dogra et al., 2001). These findings are useful material to consider when trying to understand the similarities and differences in children and young people's mental health in a diverse multi-ethnic society. Chapter 4 examines the evidence to contribute towards culturally competent practice in child and adolescent mental health, but for now the focus will be on the general ways in which the mental health of young people is conceptualised. The way in which psychiatry influences this agenda and some of the theoretical resources available to help social workers in their practice will also be examined.

Definitions and distinctions

Mental health problems are abnormalities of emotions, behaviour, or social relationships sufficiently marked or prolonged to cause suffering or risk to optimal development in the child or distress or disturbance in the family or community.
(Kurtz, 1992).

This formulation has echoes of the concept of child abuse to social workers familiar with the Children Act definition and the concept of significant harm. Note the idea of abnormality of emotions and the notion of them being sufficiently marked or prolonged. This parallel is useful in as much as it reveals how imprecise these definitions are and how open they are to interpretation. Who decides what is abnormal, the worker, parent, or child? How is the notion of sufficiently marked or prolonged measured and against what standard?

Mental health is described as 'a relative state of mind in which a person . . . is able to cope with, and adjust to, the recurrent stress of everyday living' (Anderson and Anderson, 1995). This definition of mental health introduces the idea of relativity and seems to advance the notion of coping with and adjusting to everyday living. Do black children and young people have to cope with and adjust to the everyday stress of racism? Can mental health be achieved by tolerating unemployment, poor housing, or social exclusion? Social workers practising in a psycho-social context will be attuned to the social dimension affecting children's mental health. They need to consider how they define the terms mental disorder and mental health and whether their practice aims to help children and young people 'adjust to the stress of everyday living' or challenge those stresses within a personal helping relationship.

The behaviour and emotional effect of children and young people designated with symptoms of mental illness can be considered in different ways within a variety of professional discourses. The dominant discourse is that of medicine and especially psychiatry, which continues to refine classifications of symptoms into universal descriptors (WHO, 1992; American Psychiatric Association, 1994). Yet behaviour and expressed emotions can be interpreted widely, depending on the theoretical base of the professional involved and the specific cultural and historical context of their manifestation.

'A mental disorder must cause clinically significant distress or impairment in social, occupational or other important areas of functioning' (APA, 1987). This definition was constructed in the context of a debate among psychiatrists about the criteria for diagnosing specific mental health problems. Previously they had relied on a constellation of symptoms to distinguish children and adolescents whose condition was outside the normal experience. A recent study drew attention to the limitations in psychiatric diagnosis and by implication, the medical model it embodies (Pickles et al., 2001). This study found that not all children with symptoms of mental disorder showed marked impairment, and conversely, some children had significant psycho-social impairment without reaching the clinical threshold for diagnosis.

If it is problematic to define mental *illness* or disorder, then it is equally difficult to define what is meant by mental *health* for children and young people. It can mean different things to families, children, or professionals, and staff from different professional backgrounds might not share the same perception of what mental health is. A multidisciplinary group agreed (HAS, 1995) that mental health in childhood and adolescence is indicated by:

- A capacity to enter into and sustain mutually satisfying personal relationships.
- A continuing progression of psychological development.
- An ability to play and to learn so that attainments are appropriate for age and intellectual level.
- A developing moral sense of right and wrong.
- The degree of psychological distress and maladaptive behaviour being within normal limits for the child's age and context.

Defined in this way, mental health is a rather ideal state, which depends upon the potential and experience of each individual, and is maintained or hindered by external circumstances and events. According to Hadfield (1975):

The child who is mentally healthy 'will obviously be both efficient and successful, for all his energies are employed to their full capacity. He will have a strong will and character, and be intelligent and moral.

This rather minimalist definition can be contrasted with a more fulsome contemporary definition of the HAS version offered by the Mental Health Foundation (1999) who suggest that children who are mentally healthy will have the ability to:

- Develop psychologically, emotionally, creatively, intellectually and physically.
- Initiate, develop and sustain mutually satisfying personal relationships.
- Use and enjoy solitude.
- Become aware of others and empathise with them.
- Play and learn.
- Develop a sense of right and wrong.
- Resolve (face) problems and setbacks and learn from them.

These definitions and the subtle distinctions between mental illness and mental health are important in the sense that they set the context for how social workers and others conceptualise difficulties experienced by children and young people. Examples in the last chapter showed how education, youth justice, and social work staff can all offer quite different explanations for the same behaviour with significantly different outcomes to intervention.

A nationwide survey of child mental health discovered that children under 15 years of age with obsessive-compulsive disorder were going undetected and failing to receive appropriate help despite the availability of safe and effective treatment (Heyman et al., 2001). Further evidence for the difference in professional perceptions of mental health problems is shown by another survey conducted among GPs. It revealed that they were only identifying 2 per cent of the 23 per cent of children attending GP surgeries who had some form of severe psychological or emotional problem (Mental Health Foundation, 1993). These findings are worrying because primary care is one of the most crucial gateways for children and young people to gain access to appropriate services and resources and for signposting to accessible and acceptable support in this area.

The way children and young people are characterised in popular culture or in media representations as either dangerous insatiable tearaways, or passive, angelic cherubs, captures the ambivalence in adult attitudes to children and young people. This translates into policies and practices to manage the social manifestations of childhood and adolescent experience. Essentially, this means offering punitive and restrictive, or paternalistic and patronising responses to their needs, instead of recognition of serious health needs.

It is worth bearing in mind, that it is adults who have constructed these definitions of mental health or mental health problems. There is little evidence of children or young people being consulted about how *they* define mental health or mental health problems. This is consistent with adult behaviour towards children in general, and at one level it springs from protective instincts. However, given the dominance of white, middle class males in psychiatry, it can be argued that the values they represent will be reflected in concepts of mental health problems and remain unchallenged for the most part. In so doing they will not incorporate the views, opinions, and perceptions of children themselves. This therefore risks alienating children and young people and failing to communicate with them properly about a vitally important part of their lives.

It is important to try to understand the emotional world of children and young people if assessment and intervention strategies are going to meet their needs. The vocabulary, the perceptions and the culture of emotional and behavioural difficulties that children and young people employ, need to be incorporated into the education, training and development of social workers and other staff engaged in this work. A psycho-social perspective offers a holistic tool with which to assemble all the important information about a child or young person that incorporates her or his internal as well as external context. Social work values and principles of empowerment are at the heart of good practice in child and adolescent mental health.

Prevalence and problems

Recent evidence indicates that 10 per cent of children up to the age of 18 years in Britain have a diagnosable mental health disorder. Higher rates exist among those living in inner city environments. One in five children and adolescents has a mental health problem which although less serious still requires professional support (Audit Commission, 1998; Office for National Statistics, 2001). It has been further estimated that child and adolescent mental health services are only reaching a minority of the population in their catchment areas requiring help. This indicates a large number of children and young people who are not receiving the necessary support and help to relieve their suffering. The research shows for example that one in 17 adolescents have harmed themselves, representing 200,000 11–15 year olds. At the other end of the age spectrum there are increasing numbers of children under seven years of age being excluded from school due to uncontrollable behavioural problems. The increased rate of suicide over the last twenty eight years in children and adolescents is a cause of increasing concern and a stark indicator of the mental health of young people (McClure, 2001). Table 2.1 shows the prevalence and range of specific problems affecting children at different ages, and those indicating a gender bias.

Trends in suicide are influenced by a variety of factors. One of the more

Table 2.1: Prevalence of specific child and adolescent mental health problems (DoH, 1995)

Emotional disorders	4.5–9.9% of 10 year olds
Major depression	0.5–2.5% of children, 2–8% of adolescents
Conduct disorders	6.2–10.8% of 10 year olds
Tic disorders	1–13% of boys, 1–11% of girls
Obsessive compulsive disorder	1.9% of adolescents
Hyperkinetic disorder (ADHD)	1 in 200 of all children
Encopresis (faecal soiling)	2.3% of boys, 0.7% of girls aged 7–8 years
Anorexia nervosa	0.5%–1% of 12–19 year olds
Bulimia nervosa	1% of adolescent girls and young women
Attempted suicide	2–4% of adolescents
Suicide	7.6 per 100,000 15–19 year olds
Alcohol abuse	29% of all 13 year olds drink weekly
Cannabis	3–5% of 11–16 year olds have used
Heroin and cocaine	Less than 1%
Hallucinogens	Increase reported

significant is change in the lethality and ease of availability of commonly used methods of suicide. Broadly speaking the pattern suggests that in the 1970s overdose was more common, in the 1980s carbon monoxide from car exhausts fumes, and in the 1990s death by hanging was more common. Restrictions on availability of painkillers and the fitting of catalytic converters in vehicles have affected this pattern. Actual suicide rates may be at much higher levels due to the classification by official coroners who may consider there is insufficient evidence that the injury was self-inflicted and the individual intended to die. There is also anecdotal evidence that some coroners classify some suicides as undetermined or accidental in order to spare the anguish of parents and carers.

Factors associated with suicide in young people include depression, severe mental illness and personality disorder. Also, substance misuse-particularly alcohol, predates suicidal behaviour in many cases. The sharp increase in suicides among 15 to 19 year old men recently, mirrors the period which has shown a large increase in the use of alcohol and drugs among young people generally (Appleby et al., 1999). Disrupted relationships caused by family breakdown and social exclusion in terms of unemployment are factors strongly associated with young male suicide. There is an assumption that the gender disparity in rates of suicide in young people (3 males to 1 female) reflects the changing roles of men and women in contemporary society.

This then leaves young women with higher levels of self-esteem and better coping strategies, and young men with a problematic masculine identity and an inability to acknowledge and communicate emotional difficulties (Gunnell et al., 1999). On the other hand there is evidence that changes to gender roles is having an effect on young women's capacity for externalising mental health problems with anti-social behaviour, rather than the traditional internalising of mental health problems. Between 2001 and 2002 there was a 40 per cent increase in the number of young women sentenced to secure custody (Youth Justice Board, 2002). The concept of the emotionally illiterate male is nothing new but as with all simplistic stereotypes, it obscures more than it illuminates. The startling increase in young male suicide rates cannot be explained in a generalised notion of the consequences of bottled up feelings or the empowerment of women. Nor can the dramatic increase in eating disorders among young females be consistent with the emotionally sophisticated stereotyped image that is projected. A more subtle and complex explanation is required.

Recent evidence confirms for example that suicide is of particular concern in marginalised and victimised adolescent groups including gay, lesbian, and bisexual youth. Research suggests that despite the rhetoric of anti-discriminatory policies and professional statements of equality, heterosexist and homophobic attitudes continue to be displayed by some psychologists and social workers (Morrison and L'Heureux, 2001). This can further reinforce feelings of rejection, confusion and despair in troubled young people. Other evidence warns against a narrow definition of sexual-minority adolescents that pathologises their behaviour or wrongly assumes a higher risk of self-harming behaviour (Savin-Williams, 2001).

Poverty is one factor strongly associated with child mental health problems. The prevalence for any mental disorder ranges from 16 per cent among children living in families with a gross weekly household income of under £100, to 9 per cent among children of families in the £300–£399 weekly income range. Only about 6 per cent of children and young people in those families earning £500 per week or more will suffer a mental health problem (ONS, 2001). Using this data it has been calculated that in a Primary School of 250 pupils there will be 3 children who are seriously depressed, 11 children suffering significant distress, 12 children who have phobias, and 15 children with a conduct disorder. In a typical Secondary School with 1000 pupils there will be 50 who are seriously depressed, 100 who are suffering significant distress, and 5–10 girls with an eating disorder. Many of these children will be exhibiting defensive behaviour such as aggression, poor attention, and disruption in the classroom, combined with poor attendance. They will almost certainly be seen as troublesome rather than suffering from a mental health problem thereby missing appropriate help and support.

Studies have shown that problems that begin in early childhood and remain untreated are likely to persist into later childhood and young adulthood. Parents and carers tend to assume that children will grow out of difficult behaviours and ascribe them to commonly held beliefs about normality. Phrases such as the terrible twos, childhood tantrums or adolescent turmoil enter common *parlance* and with it an unspoken assumption that these are somehow developmental milestones of a transient nature. The evidence however suggests that with conduct disorders (see below) and ADHD it is difficult to prevent the development of later anti-social activity. On the other hand, children with emotional disorders (see below) tend to be more successfully helped (Sutton, 1999).

It is useful to the discussion about definitions and distinctions to make a distinction between mental health problems, and mental health disorders (Wallace et al., 1995). *Problems* are defined as a disturbance of function in one area of relationships, mood, behaviour, or development of sufficient severity to require professional intervention. Mental health *disorders* are defined as either a severe problem, commonly persistent, or the co-occurrence of a number of problems, usually in the presence of a number of risk factors. This can be translated into some descriptions of the more common disorders of mental health found in children and adolescents:

- **Emotional disorders** (phobias, anxiety states, depression).
- **Conduct disorders** (stealing, defiance, fire-setting, aggression, anti-social behaviour).
- **Hyperkinetic disorders** (disturbance of activity and attention, ADHD).
- **Developmental disorders** (autism, speech delay, poor bladder control).
- **Eating disorders** (infant eating problems, anorexia nervosa, bulimia).
- **Habit disorders** (tics, sleeping problems, soiling).
- **Somatic disorders** (chronic fatigue syndrome).
- **Psychotic disorders** (schizophrenia, manic depression, drug-induced psychoses).

The latter disorder represents one of the most serious, rare, and controversial disorders classified by psychiatrists. Until relatively recently, child and adolescent psychiatrists had previously considered that the onset of schizophrenia only occurred in late adolescence. However, there is growing evidence that younger children are experiencing this most severe form of mental health problem without receiving adequate help and support (Remschmidt, 2001). Part of the reason for this is the general reluctance to diagnose such a disorder because of fears about the potentially adverse consequences of the label. But there is also a history of uncertainty and lack of reliable classification instruments with which to apply a core definition across the variety of childhood developmental stages.

Understandings and causes

In considering the various ways in which children's mental health is understood by professionals it is useful to consider some of the theoretical and research-based evidence on human growth and development, social policy, and sociology as part of the repertoire of guidance available. Social workers are expected to have a sound grounding in these subjects to help inform all aspects of their work with a range of service user age groups. The theories are vast and to do them justice would require more space than this text permits. Some of the classic authors and contemporary literature will be referred to. However, there are some fundamental principles and elements that can be utilised to help illuminate the area of child and adolescent mental health and social work practice.

A good starting point is in a sense where some of the theories end. Wherever the emphasis is placed on the spectrum of the nature versus nurture debate and any explanation for human behaviour in the literature, social workers need to be clear where *they place themselves* as individuals. Not for the purpose of trying to prove a theory right or to convince themselves of the correct explanation for the behaviour of a child or young person, but to make more explicit their own personal bias. This is not a weakness but a strength. A social worker knowing where they stand and understanding there are other perceptions and beliefs about a child, and adopting an inquisitive, flexible stance, will be acting in the child's best interests. Rather that, than trying to defend the indefensible or answer the unanswerable.

Recent advances in genetic research and refinement of developmental instruments for assessing children and young people's emotional and behavioural health have concluded that to regard nature and nurture as separate and independent is an oversimplification. The answer to what shapes children and adolescents' mental health is both nature and the environment, or rather, the interplay between the two.

Whether the ideas of Freud, Klein, Piaget, Eriksen, Skinner, or Bowlby and others help or hinder the process of work, the important point is that it permits the adoption of some intellectual rigour to the way the work is organised (Mills and Duck, 2000; Beckett, 2002). This can provide a framework within which the selection of assessment and intervention methods and models can take place. Crucially, it will enable a more systematic process to proceed in a recognisable direction or provide a knowledge base to discuss ideas put forward by other staff. This will be helpful in case conferences, legal proceedings, or report writing contexts. Sometimes it is helpful to acknowledge that there is no clear-cut explanation, or there are multiple interpretations for a child's emotional and behavioural problems that are concerning others.

Social workers with a psycho-social perspective can especially utilise theoretical concepts from social policy and sociology to add to their framework of explanation. This distinguishes the social work contribution from most other agency staff in child mental health work. The combination can be powerful, adding weight to professional arguments and provide authority for interpretations. They can also be burdensome and confusing and should therefore always be used cautiously. They enable a social model of mental health to be acknowledged alongside others. The choice is again vast in the area of sociology alone. Marx, Durkheim, Mills, Parsons, Popper, or Habermas and others, offer a rich and diverse knowledge base (O'Donnell, 2002). The important point is that the chosen theoretical preference can be identified and acknowledged, and a plan can proceed consistently within that premise. Chapter 7 examines some key resources in more detail.

The importance of reflective practice whilst undertaking work with children and adolescents cannot be emphasised enough. In the process of using measures of human growth and development it is crucial. This is because children and young people are constantly changing as are their circumstances. This requires a high level of concentration and alertness to changes that will be unique and unpredictable, as well as changes that appear to conform to a predictable developmental transition. Such changes may have nothing to do with social work intervention and some may have everything to do with it. The key is in appreciating that developmental issues are significant and require social workers to have a good grasp of them (Thompson, 2002).

The following chapter aims to help the harnessing of these intellectual resources in deciding what to do in working with troubled children and young people. For now, summaries of the key elements of human growth and development theoretical resources relevant to CAMHS are assembled below. They have been simplified to aid clarity and comparison and should be seen as part of a wide spectrum of potential, rather than deterministic, interactive causative factors in the genesis of child and adolescent mental health problems. Some social psychologists criticise the emphasis in child development theories on normative concepts and suggest enhancing the judging, measuring approach towards one that embodies context, culture, and competencies (Woodhead, 1998). The following summaries should be adapted to every individual situation encountered and always considered against the white, Eurocentric perceptions they embodied when first constructed.

Developmental theories and resources

Eriksens psycho-social stages of development:

Five of Eriksen's eight stages of development will be considered.

Year 1: The infant requires consistent and stable care in order to develop feelings of security. Begins to trust the environment but can also develop suspicion and insecurity. Deprivation at this stage can lead to emotional detachment throughout life and difficulties forming relationships.

Years 2–3: The child begins to explore and seeks some independence from parents/carers. A sense of autonomy develops but improved self-esteem can combine with feelings of shame and self-doubt. Failure to integrate at this stage may lead to difficulties in social integration.

Years 4–5: The child needs to explore the wider environment and plan new activities. Begins to initiate activities but fears punishment and guilt as a consequence. Successful integration results in a confident person, but problems can produce deep insecurities.

Years 6–11: The older child begins to acquire knowledge and skills to adapt to surroundings. Develops sense of achievement but marred by possible feelings of inferiority and failure if efforts are denigrated.

Years 12–18: The individual enters stage of personal and vocational identity formation. Self perception heightened, but potential for conflict, confusion, and strong emotions.

Freuds psychosexual stages of development:

Year 1: The oral stage during which the infant obtains its' principle source of comfort from sucking the breast milk of the mother, and the gratification from the nutrition.

Years 2–3: The anal stage when the anus and defecation are the major sources of sensual pleasure. The child is preoccupied with body control with parental/carer encouragement. Obsessional behaviour and over-control later in childhood could indicate a problematic stage development.

Years 4–5: The phallic stage, with the penis the focus of attention is the characteristic of this psychosexual stage. In boys the oedipus complex and in girls the electra complex are generated in desires to have a sexual relationship with the opposite sex parent. The root of anxieties and neuroses can be found here if transition to the next stage is impeded.

Years 6–11: The latency stage, which is characterised by calm after the storm of the powerful emotions preceding it.

Years 12–18: The genital stage whereby the individual becomes interested in opposite-sex partners as a substitute for the opposite-sex parent, and as a way of resolving the tensions inherent in oedipul and electra complexes.

Bowlbys attachment theory:

The following scheme represents the process of healthy attachment formation. Mental health problems may develop if an interruption occurs in this process, if care is inconsistent, or if there is prolonged separation from main carer.

Months 0–2: This stage is characterised by pre-attachment undiscriminating social responsiveness. The baby is interested in voices and faces and enjoys social interaction.

Months: 3–6: The infant begins to develop discriminating social responses and experiments with attachments to different people. Familiar people elicit more response than strangers.

Months 7–36: Attachment to main carer is prominent with the child showing separation anxiety when carer is absent. The child actively initiates responses from the carer.

Years 3–18: The main carers' absences become longer, but the child develops a reciprocal attachment relationship. The child and developing young person begins to understand the carers' needs from a secure emotional base.

Piagets stages of cognitive development:

Years 0–1½: The sensory-motor stage characterised by infants exploring their physicality and modifying reflexes until they can experiment with objects and builds a mental picture of things around them.

Years 1½–7: The pre-operational stage when the child acquires language, makes pictures, and participates in imaginative play. The child tends to be self-centred and fixed in her/his thinking believing they are responsible for external events.

Years 7–12: The concrete operations stage when a child can understand and apply more abstract tasks such as sorting or measuring. This stage is characterised by less egocentric thinking and more relational thinking-differentiation between things. The complexity of the external world is beginning to be appreciated.

Years 12–18: The stage of formal operations characterised by the use of rules and problem-solving skills. The child moves into adolescence with increasing capacity to think abstractly and reflect on tasks in a deductive, logical way.

A more recent view of personality development lists five factors that combine elements of the older more classic ways of understanding a child or adolescent together with notions of peer acceptability and adult perceptions (Hampson, 1995; Jones and Jones, 1999):

- **Extroversion** – includes traits such as extroverted/introverted, talkative/quiet, bold/timid
- **Agreeableness** – based on characteristics such as agreeable/disagreeable, kind/unkind, selfish/unselfish
- **Conscientiousness** – reflects traits such as organised/disorganised, hardworking/lazy, reliable/unreliable, thorough/careless, practical/impractical
- **Neuroticism** – based on traits such as stable/unstable, calm/angry, relaxed/tense, unemotional/emotional
- **Openness to experience** – includes the concept of intelligence, together with level of sophistication, creativity, curiosity and cognitive style in problem-solving situations

Sociological perspectives

In addition to the classic means of understanding child and adolescent development outlined above there are other, less prominent but as important resources for social workers to draw upon to help inform practice in this area. Sociology may be suffering from less emphasis in government policy and occupational standards guidance but it still offers a valuable conceptual tool to enable a rounded, holistic process of assessment and intervention. Sociological explanations for child and adolescent mental health problems can be located in a *macro* understanding of the way childhood itself is considered and constructed by adults (James and Prout, 1990):

- Childhood is a social construction. It is neither a natural nor a universal feature of human groups but appears as a specific structural and cultural component of many societies.
- Childhood is a variable of social analysis. Comparative and cross-cultural analysis reveals a variety of childhoods rather than a single or universal phenomenon.
- Children's social relationships and cultures require study in their own right, independent of the perspective and concern of adults.
- Children are and must be seen as active in the construction and determination of their own lives, the lives of those around them and of the societies in which they live.

An examination of the experience of childhood around the world today shows how greatly varied it is, and how it has changed throughout history. Contemporary children in some countries are working from the ages of eight and independent from the age of 14, whereas in other countries some do not leave home or begin work until they are 21 (Alderson, 2000; Hendrick, 1997; Bilton et al., 2002). The developmental norms above show how adults construct childhood and therefore how to measure children's progress and detect mental health problems. They are however set down as solid absolutes and are based on notions of adults' fears about risk, lack of confidence in children, and rooted in adults' own childhood experiences. These theories have had positive effects but they have also restricted the field of vision required to fully engage with and understand children and adolescents.

Early childhood studies are beginning to challenge the orthodoxy in child development theories so that children are seen as accomplishing, living, competent persons rather than not yet quite fully formed people who are learning to become adults (Early Childhood Education Forum, 1998). The idea that the stages have to be accomplished sequentially ignores the different pace different children change according to external and other influences. Adults simply need to reflect on themselves to see that adults of the same developmental age can be at very different stages of emotional maturity, skill and capacity. Social workers therefore need to use concepts of development and definitions of child and adolescent mental health problems cautiously and sceptically. An appreciation of how these concepts are constructs reflecting historical and cultural dominant values, and how they reinforce the power relationships between adults and children, is required.

Social workers and other professionals in the field of child and adolescent mental health need to demonstrate and incorporate in routine practice an element of intellectual modesty. This can be difficult when workloads are increasing and demands on time are enormous, or there appears to be a risky situation to deal with. It is also hard to admit to not knowing or being confused or uncertain – these are not what managers, the public and policy makers expect. Yet they may be realistic and a more accurate picture than presenting a neat, coherent explanation for a child's behaviour in a short time scale. The competitive power dynamics in inter-agency meetings or high-pressured conferences cannot tolerate ambiguity; they demand clarity, brevity and certainty. However, hasty judgements made to protect embarrassment or personal vulnerability can have long-term consequences.

Preventive practice

It is important not to be overly influenced by the negative connotations of causes, definitions and consequences. Too much emphasis on spotting emerging or established mental health problems can distract from the critically important social work role of prevention. The literature on preventive work in child and adolescent mental health is extensive and in later chapters, specific measures will be examined for their usefulness in the context of evidence-based practice consistent with social work principles, values and national occupational standards. For now, some general theoretical concepts will be described and discussed in order to locate the position of social work practice in the debate about definitions of mental health, before moving into Chapter 3 which considers the importance of social work assessment of children and young people's mental health problems.

An ecological paradigm that understands the individual person in an interactive relationship with their particular environment is a helpful point of departure in seeking to explain the internal and external stresses producing mental health problems. A health education framework that tackles the consequences of drug and alcohol misuse, combined with targeted early intervention and provision of accessible services in high-risk groups, is another important factor. Thirdly, given the significance in interpersonal problems as precipitating factors in the triggering of mental health difficulties, life skills education and training should be emphasised at known developmental crisis points such as pre-adolescence (Hawton et al., 1998).

Prevention is better than cure. One of the difficulties in engaging children and young people as well as others in preventive practice is the stigma and prejudice attached to mental health problems. The statistics show how relatively common these problems are, and how very common for the less severe conditions or mild forms. Yet the phenomenon is either cloaked in secrecy with people ashamed to admit to suffering in this way, or it is portrayed in dramatic, dangerous and disturbing imagery. In the context of children and young people it gets mixed together with other notions reflecting the demonisation and denigration of young people.

This is a powerful cocktail of ideas, and in the hands of a generally irresponsible media it can feed the general public with distorted or unrealistic perceptions of child mental health problems. Further stigmatisation can occur when mental health problems are linked with aggression, criminality, and unpredictability. This can exaggerate public fears about young people with mental health problems. Also people find it easier to see mental health problems belonging to others rather than themselves or their children. This protects against powerful feelings of vulnerability and that most threatening of ideas – that *everyone* is capable of becoming mentally unwell (Dogra et al., 2001).

The task of preventive practice is not made easier if the notion of a continuum between mental health and mental disorder is accepted. This means that the dividing line between mental health and disorder is difficult to define. Anxiety before important events such as school examinations is natural. But at what point does the anxiety become overwhelming or problematic enough to warrant specific help from professionals? There can be unwillingness for some children and young people to recognise that some distress is a component of the human experience. This need not require being defined as a mental health problem and can be tackled in other more appropriate ways. Equally, there are parents/carers and professionals for whom the concept of mental health problems in young children is hard to grasp. Social workers are ideally positioned at the interface between health and social care with a community focus to their work, to engage in demystifying and challenging the stigma and prejudice associated with child and adolescent mental health problems.

Social workers will be familiar with the concept of risk assessment and its more active counterpart, risk management. When addressing the mental health needs of children and young people there are some helpful guidelines available to weigh up potential risk factors during the process of identification of problems. As in other risk assessment contexts social workers will be evaluating a variety of sources of information about a client from all those in contact with the young person. It has already been acknowledged that one of the first skills to bring to these situations is that of understanding that a child's behaviour may be perceived and described in a number of different ways, according to the values, knowledge base, and training of the individual providing the information. Social workers then need to be able to sift this data and incorporate their own model of mental health in order to produce a useful working definition.

Using anti-racist and anti-discriminatory principles social workers can also reflect on how conceptualisations of normal and abnormal behaviours, and attitudes towards mental health, will vary in different cultural groups. An understanding of the racism and prejudice impacting on the lives of Black children will assist in the most appropriate assessment and intervention strategies being deployed. Broadly speaking, in Western industrialised cultures the development of independence and self-reliance is highly valued, whereas in many Black cultures the idea of group interdependence and co-operation is considered important. In Chinese families self-control and composure can be idealised and the expression of emotion frowned upon.

In some cultures mental illness is believed to be a punishment from the Gods, or a hereditary weakness. Consequently, somatic symptoms are likely to mask mental health problems and be overlooked. A culturally competent approach to child and adolescent mental health problems will take account of the fact that for many people in Britain's diverse multi-cultural communities, mental health problems may be presented as physical illness. A narrow psychiatric diagnosis of mental disorder may in fact be normal behaviour within a particular cultural group. Chapter 4 examines the topic of culturally competent practice in further detail.

The psycho-social approach forming the core of social work practice enables social workers to focus on the social factors often neglected or underplayed by other professional staff and parents/carers. Combining this with culturally competent practice is a powerful antidote to the medicalised and psychiatric influence in child and adolescent mental health services. It is not possible to be definitive about the risks of developing mental health problems or the sequence of causation. A significant review of the association between environmental stressors with the physical and psychological health of children provides strong evidence for the need to adopt a holistic psycho-social framework for understanding the context of child and adolescent mental health problems (Grey, 1993).

Examples included the depressive symptoms of children with chronic physical illness or disability, emotional and behavioural problems in deaf children, and low self-esteem in children suffering with asthma. The psychiatric literature in child and adolescent mental health is relatively young and sociological or genetic/biological explanations are still developing in this field. However, as noted above, there is evidence that particular groups of children and young people are more vulnerable than most. Chapter 3 looks at this in more detail but for now some of the background social and environmental characteristics that can be related to the contemporary increase in children's mental health problems reveal that Britain has:

- Among the worst pre-school provision in Europe.
- Highest rate of teenage pregnancy in Europe.
- Highest rate of under-age alcohol abuse in Europe.
- Among the lowest rate of further and higher education take-up in Europe.

- Highest rate of child poverty in comparable European countries.
- Highest rate of childhood asthma in Europe.

(Sources: ONS, DoH, CPAG, DfEE, EEC).

This selective sample of characteristics in comparison to the rest of Europe is included to provide a feel for the kind of experiences children and adolescents are having. They show that while there is statistical uniformity in prevalence rates for mental health problems across Europe and North America, nevertheless in Britain it is possible to gain a depth of understanding of those factors that may be influencing emotional and behavioural development. It should be born in mind of course that this sample may represent some of those characteristics *caused by* mental health problems. Above all they reinforce the importance of the need for a social dimension to practice in this area and always to consider a genetic/biological component.

Social workers have a mandate to work with children and young people who feel alienated, unloved, discriminated against, marginalised and impoverished. The evidence demonstrates that children from every class background, gender and culture are at risk of developing mental health problems. Some are more vulnerable than others while the causes for their difficulties could be as diverse as their individual personalities and circumstances. A pro-active child-focused, community oriented practice that takes children seriously and is cognisant of the potential adverse circumstances responsible for triggering problems, is likely to be more rather than less helpful. The specific elements of this form of social work intervention will be discussed in Chapter 5, but the key principles in beginning to understand whether or why a child or young person is, or may be developing mental health problems are:

- Harness a variety of explanatory theoretical resources rather than rely on one.
- Be aware that different professionals have different perceptions of the same phenomena.
- Develop a psycho-social holistic approach which includes environmental factors.
- Resist stereotyping cultural and behavioural attributes.
- Acknowledge that theories of childhood are adult constructs.
- Consider the impact and stigma attached to a diagnosis of mental health disorder.
- Be aware of the power of the medical model and psychiatric professionals.
- Balance the need for normalisation with the potential to deny serious problems.

Summary of key points

Definitions of mental illness or mental health are fluid concepts. Social workers need to be aware of the theoretical basis for such definitions and the distinctions between them. Psychiatry is the dominant profession in CAMHS but only through historical accident and the power and status of the medical establishment. Children's perceptions and their own constructions of their emotional status are absent from the medical literature.

Theories of child and adolescent development are based on white ethno-centric norms of psychological development and behaviour. These resources should be used with caution and adapted to the cultural context of the child and family encountered and with regard to their experiences of institutional and personal racism.

Poverty as a factor in the prevalence of child and adolescent mental health problems is strongly indicated but is not deterministic. Boys tend to externalise problems and girls internalise problems. This has led to a rapid increase in completed suicide in young men aged 15–24 years of age, and increased rates of eating disorders in young females, although recent research suggests the gender specivity of these problems is diminishing.

Social workers need to contribute towards preventive practice and help reduce the stigma attached to mental health problems, enabling children and young people to seek help before a small problem becomes a large one. Drawing on those theoretical resources most useful to the particular person being helped is better than using one theory universally. Sociological theories concerning the construction of childhood are a useful addition to the medical literature on CAMHS.

CHAPTER 3

Assessing and Understanding

Introduction

Social workers special contribution to CAMHS work is in their unique capacity to hold onto the external reality-the *context* of the whole family experience. The capacity to stay with the pain of each family's situation, to see the patterns and sequences evolving, and to assess the impact of social policy and political changes on children and their families. A psycho-social perspective can permit a historical analysis of how children have been differently understood and portrayed in various epochs, combined with evaluation of the local, current, familial and interpersonal pattern of relationships shaping their existence.

A significant imperative to consider for any sociological understanding of childhood and mental health problems encountered during that phase of development is that the child is always revealing of the grounds of social control. In other words do we get the children we deserve? How much does the environment children and young people grow up in determine their emotional and behavioural state? Any social work assessment of a child or young person needs to locate the start of the assessment process in the context of an understanding of the historical perspectives on normality in childhood that constantly reflect the changes in the organisation of the social structure of society (Jenks, 1996).

Children have been disregarded, exploited, or traded in earlier epochs, and the Victorian notion of children being seen but not heard still resonates today in some of the populist social commentaries. Children's mental health problems are particularly difficult for social thinkers who of course are parents/carers themselves, because it involves thinking differently about children and young people. It also means consciously or unconsciously revisiting their own childhood. The heritage of perceptions of children's behaviour and emotions still provides material for constructing children as little demons possessed by primitive urges. Or they are perceived as uncontrollable manipulators, proto-adults, and juvenile delinquents. On the other hand they are seen as precious, fragile, full of goodness little angels without a bad thought in their head. All of these ideas try to account for the phenomenon of childhood, generally speaking, without addressing the potential for mental health explanations. The concept of children having rights as citizens and needs defined in their terms is still relatively new, and for some people a cause for barely-disguised consternation (Treseder, 1997).

Durkheim provides some clues to his perception of childhood and how social workers might be feeling when embarking on an assessment-whether formal or informal – in the area of child and adolescent mental health:

Whichever stage in the period of childhood chosen for consideration, one is always confronted with an intelligence which is at one and the same time so weak and fragile, so newly-formed and delicately constituted, endowed with such limited faculties and acting, as it were, in such a miraculous way. One cannot help trembling with fear, when one gives the matter thought, for the safety of this delightful but fragile mechanism.   (cited in Pickering, 1979).

These words capture something of the emotional paralysis often experienced by social workers when presented with a child or young person causing concern. There is fear of saying or doing the wrong thing in case it makes matters worse, as well as ambivalence leading to a desire to restrain, intervene strongly, or enforce control over the behaviour being exhibited. It is very important before embarking on work in this area that the social worker is aware of their feelings in order that they do not get in the way of understanding the client. By monitoring these feelings the social worker can maximise the opportunities offered by the encounter to absorb information and provide the basis for change and development.

Social workers may bring expectations to the encounter of being helpful, kind, and tolerant, even more so if the child or young person is the victim of neglect, abuse, or social exclusion. However, tolerance towards destructiveness, aggression, or anti-social behaviour needs to be distinguished between appeasement or collusion and the ability to acknowledge the underlying feelings and being able to bear them. If the social worker communicates fear and denial by glossing over or excusing the client's feelings, then the child will also be unable to bear and manage the despair, depression or hostility inside them (Salzberger-Wittenberg, 1981).

Principles underlying assessment

A developmental approach to assessment in child and adolescent mental health is a helpful base from which to build up a picture of the problem being presented and the prospects for appropriate intervention (Rutter et al., 1994). Children behave differently at different ages and some broad understanding of the range of expected behaviours expected at each age can assist in judging the nature of the problem. It is also useful to assess the severity of the problem by considering how far the course of psychological development has been interrupted. The theoretical resources to assist in this task were reviewed in Chapter 2 along with discussion of their cultural and social limitations. However there are some general principles that can, albeit cautiously, be applied.

Different phases of development are associated with different stresses and susceptibilities, which must be taken into account during assessment. For example very young children are prone to adverse reactions to hospital admission, or prolonged separation, while adolescents can be vulnerable to profound depressive mood swings. If social workers are to understand how problems have arisen they must clarify, or seek access to expertise that can help explain and distinguish what is normal from what is not. Normal in this sense means normal to that of a similar child, in that situation from that culture. Equally, it is important to disentangle direct and indirect effects and linking events, capacities and behaviours. Outcomes can be mediated or moderated by other concurrent factors.

It is not just individual children's capacities that are important but also the content of emotions and relationships. The timing of experiences influences their impact because of the stage of psychological capacity that are emerging and the relevance such as the response of others. There may be continuities and discontinuities in outward behaviour which need to be understood in the context of continuity and discontinuity in the environment. It is insufficient to know that major life events such as starting school, the birth of a sibling, or leaving home have occurred. It is crucial to understand individual differences in the meaning attached to such transitions (Cox, 1994).

The risk in relying on generalisations and assumptions about normality is that social workers will condense knowledge into pragmatic and quickly available guidelines to their practice. This can result in stereotyping, superficial assessment, and lead to inflexible, routinised practice. On the other hand trying to juggle all the infinite number of variables, nuances, distinctions, and disparate factors involved in a child or young person's experience is likely to lead to unhelpful paralysis. Accessing a diverse range of opinion, reviewing judgements, testing hypotheses, and bearing some uncertainty can help in this complex work. Each situation is unique and so is each individual social worker. Therefore the development of personal insight is crucial for the social worker involved.

Interviewing children and young people

Some of the theoretical frameworks to understanding children and the problems they might develop have been reviewed in the first two chapters. They try to help make sense of otherwise unexplained phenomena but the way they are employed and the extent to which they are useful, must be decided by each individual social worker. To a great extent this will be determined by the degree of insight and perceptiveness available within the social worker. These are some of the attitudes that can foster better communication with troubled children and young people (Salzberger-Wittenberg, 1981; Alderson, 1995; Dogra et al., 2002):

- **Providing a suitable setting**: whether in an office, clinic, school, community centre, or family home it is important to ensure that the environment is welcoming, comfortable with age-appropriate communication materials such as crayons, pens, paper, modelling clay, and puppets, available. This includes accessible materials for disabled children, and interpreters. Always sit beside rather than opposite the child or young person-it is less intimidating. Minimise distractions or interruptions.

- **Planning the session**: consent and confidentiality issues need to be considered thoroughly in accordance with child protection guidelines and the legal rights of the child. These were discussed thoroughly in Chapter 1, and need to be acknowledged openly with the client. More important than the factual position is that the proper tone is adopted when explaining the limits to confidentiality. These ideas must be seen as enabling rather than restricting communication.

- **Setting boundaries**: clarify some ground rules for the conduct of the meeting and invite the client to contribute their own preferences such as having a mid-session break or time out. Ensure the child or young person knows they can interrupt, question, or seek clarification over any concerns throughout the encounter. Explain how the work will proceed, what is expected from them, how long the meeting will last and how often.

- **Curiosity and open-mindedness**: try to reduce the influence of previous reports or assessments about the client as facts and opinions can get mixed up. Files or referral information can be inaccurate, out of date, and inhibit spontaneity and receptivity. Observation and listening skills are at a premium. Approaching the interview with the attitude of an explorer taking account of every clue, and viewing the child as a unique individual will provide the optimum foundation for understanding and establishing a trusting relationship.

- **Listening and reflecting**: non-verbal communication may be as important as the outright hostility and abusive aggression expressed by some children. The social worker adopting a procedural or questioning service-led model of assessment is unlikely to engage successfully with the client. More listening, acceptance of, and reflecting the way the child or young person feels about themselves and others will form the basis for a helping professional relationship. Reflecting is a crucial skill. An element of reframing may be necessary but this should not come across as contradiction or dismissiveness.

- **Empathy and intuition**: social workers believe it is important to put themselves into the shoes of the client. It is a familiar concept in social work practice. This empathy is considered a pre-requisite to competent, empowering practice. However it can be an unreliable guide to informing social workers of how the child or young person is feeling. A more useful attitude is to wait and be receptive to the feelings experienced during the encounter. This is not free-floating intuition but measured, systematic, intuitive practice. The psychodynamic literature explains this process more deeply, but in this context it is appropriate to simply understand that these feelings can tell much about how the child or young person is feeling and therefore how best to proceed to help (Rogers, 1975; Yelloly, 1980; Trowell and Bower, 1995).

Risk factors

The evidence suggests that interplay between characteristics in the child and their environment increase the risks of developing mental health problems. Social workers ought to find this paradigm fits with a holistic psycho-social framework for assessment and intervention. The risk factors commonly identified as indicators of potential child mental health problems included in Table 3.1 illustrates the three areas where risk factors can be identified:

Table 3.1: Factors that are known to increase the risk of mental health problems in children and young people (Audit Commission, 1998)

Child risk factors:
- genetic influences
- low IQ and learning disability
- specific developmental delay
- communication difficulty
- difficult temperament
- physical illness, especially if chronic and/or neurological
- academic failure
- low self-esteem

Family risk situations:
- overt parental conflict
- family breakdown
- inconsistent or unclear discipline
- hostile and rejecting relationships
- failure to adapt to a child's changing developmental needs
- abuse – physical, sexual and/or emotional
- parental psychiatric illness
- parental criminality, alcoholism, and personality disorder
- death and loss – including loss of friendships

Environmental risk factors:
- socio-economic disadvantage
- homelessness
- disaster
- discrimination
- other significant life events

The rise in drug and substance abuse, alcohol consumption and the widening gap between rich and poor all contribute to a fertile environment for risk factors to escalate (Townsend, 1993). The risks to children from parents with mental health problems are well understood, yet there is still evidence of a lack of liaison between adult and child and adolescent mental health services which would better serve all the family members (Howe, 1999; Parsloe, 1999; Hetherington and Baistow, 2001). Further evidence is provided in the case of suspected Munchausen's Syndrome By Proxy (MSBP) where social workers are often in conflict with paediatricians who seek to initiate care proceedings because they suspect a parent is deliberately harming their child. This can jeopardise the sensitive and critical need for joint working and a coherent holistic strategy which also addresses the mental health needs of the parent.

Social workers tend to feel intimidated by high status doctors pushing for a course of action in child protection strategy meetings, even though the evidence base for such action is wafer thin. Controversial situations involving diagnoses of ME or Autism following medical certainty about MSBP, have resulted in new guidelines being issued by the Department of Health which highlight the importance of independent assessment by social workers (DoH, 2001). Risk assessment in the context of child protection tends to focus on the likelihood of a parent harming a child in the future. This usually takes place after an incident has already occurred with the aim of preventing a recurrence, or identifying those families where harm is likely to take place (Parsloe, 1999).

Preventive and predictive risk assessment aims to target support services early enough to reach those most in need. However this process can be discriminatory, inaccurate, and statistically unreliable. Poor families and socially excluded people can feel persecuted (Dingwall, 1989). Checklists of predictive factors have led to the construction of characteristics of parents more likely to harm their children. They imply that it is only in socially disadvantaged families where abuse is more likely to take place, or that single parents, those abused in childhood, or fostered and adopted children are likely to abuse their own children. This is inaccurate, unhelpful and potentially dangerous (Parsloe, 1999).

The evidence for the effectiveness of risk assessments is not reassuring. A study of risk assessment models in the United States which mirror principles enshrined in UK guidance found that there was too high a rate of error in them, and that social workers tended to standardise practice at the expense of employing wider risk assessment methods (Lyons et al., 1996). The current norms of risk assessment are still based on white, middle class, gendered ideology. The tools of risk assessment tend not to take account of cultural factors in their construction or interpretation. There is considerable pressure on social workers and their managers to make safe decisions, which can be judged as such before and after the event. Such an impossible task leads to defensive practice and the neglect of child mental health problems, which are hard to quantify.

Resilience factors

Children with several identified risk factors demonstrate resilience and do not develop mental health problems. As well as understanding why some children develop mental health problems, it is crucially important to learn more about those who in similar circumstances do not. Research is required to analyse the nature of these resilient children to understand whether coping strategies or skills can be transferred to other children. Positive factors such as reduced social isolation, good schooling, and supportive adults outside the family appear to help. These are the very factors missing in asylum seekers, refugees, and other ethnic minority families who live in deprived conditions and suffer more socio-economic disadvantages than other children. Certain key factors appear to promote resilience in young people to mental health problems and disorders:

- Self-esteem, sociability and autonomy
- Family compassion, warmth, and absence of parental discord
- Social support systems that encourage personal effort and coping

Mental health problems frequently present in children and young people who are causing concern to staff working in education, social services, or in youth justice contexts. The capability of teachers, social workers, and probation officers, and the capacity of the services within which they work to identify these mental health problems are crucial. Chapter 6 discusses in more detail how to improve inter-professional care in this area. Being able to respond in a timely and appropriate manner to the early signs of mental health problems, may make all the difference to the chance of effective intervention for the young person. There remain however, barriers to the development of wider and better understanding of mental health difficulties among and between professionals in all agencies coming into contact with troubled children. These include:

- A widespread reluctance to 'label' a child or young person as mentally ill.
- A poor appreciation of what specialist child psychology and psychiatry services can do.
- The ways in which priorities are set within the statutory framework of the Mental Health Act 1983, Children Act 1989 and the Education Act 1993.
- Lack of knowledge and close working between agencies.

Assessment methodology in specialist child and adolescent mental health services tends to remain rooted in psychiatric diagnostic models with psycho-social factors included as risk factors reflecting negative, deficit indicators. Or, as Laing said:

This psychiatric medical model has been taken on trust even by psychiatrists until recently. This model in my view is treacherous. It is in essence anti-social. It helps us see what is going on about as much as dark glasses in an already darkened room.   (Laing, 1969).

Social workers need to embrace a more holistic approach seeking to identify and amplify strengths, coping strategies, alternative community resources, and user perceptions. It has been established that a confluence of several risk factors in childhood can create the conditions for later psycho-social difficulty, including socio-economic disadvantage, child abuse, and parental mental illness. However, there are protective mechanisms that can mitigate the chance of some children going on to develop anti-social behaviour or serious mental health problems.

A thorough assessment of risk *and* resilience factors is advocated (Rutter, 1985). These include the child's response to stress being determined by the capacity to appraise and attach meaning to their situation. Age-related susceptibilities that permit older children to use their greater understanding compared to younger children need to be understood. How a child deals with adversity either actively or reactively, and the ability to act positively, is a function of self-esteem and feelings of self-efficacy rather than indicating any inherent problem-solving skills. Features as varied as secure stable affectionate relationships, success, achievement, and temperamental attributes can foster such cognitive capacity.

These personal qualities seem to be operative as much in their effects on interactions with and responses from other people, as in their role in regulating individual responses to life events. Coping successfully with stressful situations can be a strengthening experience and promotes resilience, which can allow self-confidence to increase. Rutter (ibid) concludes that protection does not lie in the buffering effects of some supportive factor. Rather, all the evidence points towards the importance of developmental links. The quality of a child's resilience to developing mental health problems or emotional and behavioural difficulties is influenced by early life experiences but is not determinative of later outcomes.

This highlights the importance of assessment methods that take account of not just individual characteristics within the child but equally within the family and broader environment. In combination these protective factors may create a chain of indirect links that foster escape from adversity. Organising services across the spectrum of multi-agency provision in partnership between social work professionals and parents, offers the opportunity to bring out dormant protective factors to interrupt the causal chain of negative events (Little and Mount, 1999). A progressive, preventive environment that promotes children's emotional well-being is preferable to reacting to the consequences of neglect or abuse.

Individual factors regarded as promoting resilience include:

- An even and adaptable temperament.
- A capacity for problem-solving.
- Physical attractiveness.
- A sense of humour.
- Good social skills and supportive peers.
- A sense of autonomy and purpose.

- Secure attachment to at least one parent.
- Links with the wider community.

Child and family social work

Services geared towards the needs of specific age groups of children or young people, or adults can determine the type of help offered and whether it is perceived as family or individual support. The range of potential interventions is reviewed in Chapter 5. The choice of intervention becomes particularly important in the area of child and adolescent mental health where the initial assessment of the presenting problem could be formulated on an individual or family basis. Various theoretical resources can guide practical or therapeutic interventions with the individual, parents or whole family. These enable social workers to work conjointly with another social worker or another professional with different parts of the same family.

Social workers in child and family contexts are rarely short of advice, guidance, procedures, or legislative injunctions. The latest – *The Framework for the Assessment of Children in Need* – seeks to help in the task of assessment and advises combining three domains – family and environmental, parental capacity and child developmental needs, in a thorough evaluation to assist in guiding future interventions. The interaction or the influence of these domains on each other requires careful exploration during assessment. Some of the ingredients of each dimension are provided below (DoH, 2000):

The dimensions of a child's developmental needs:

- **Health** – growth, development, physical and mental well-being, genetic factors, disability, diet, exercise, immunisations, sex education, substance misuse.
- **Education** – play and interaction, books, skills, interests, achievements, school, special educational needs.
- **Emotional and Behavioural Development** – appropriateness of responses, expression of feelings, actions, attachments, temperament, adaptability, self-control, stress responses.
- **Identity** – self-perception, abilities, self-image, self-esteem, individuality, race, religion, age, gender, sexuality, disability, sense of belonging, acceptance.
- **Family and Social Relationships** – empathy, affectionate relationships, siblings, friendships.
- **Social Presentation** – appearance, behaviour, understanding of social self, dress, cleanliness, personal hygiene, use of advice.
- **Self Care Skills** – acquisition of competencies, independence, practical skills, confidence, problem solving, vulnerabilities, impact of disability.

The dimensions of parenting capacity:

- **Basic Care** – providing for physical needs, medical care, food, hygiene, warmth, shelter, clothing, hygiene.
- **Ensuring Safety** – protecting child from abuse, harm or danger, unsafe adults, self-harm, recognition of hazards.
- **Emotional Warmth** – meeting emotional needs, racial and cultural identity, valued, secure, stable and affectionate relationships, responsive to child's needs, praise, warm regard, encouragement and physical comfort.
- **Stimulation** – cognitive stimulation, intellectual development, promoting social opportunities, interaction, communication, talking, encouraging questions, play, school attendance, enabling success.
- **Guidance and Boundaries** – help guide emotions and behaviour, demonstrating and modelling behaviour and interactions with others, setting boundaries, moral development, respect own values, anger management, consideration for others, discipline.
- **Stability** – maintain secure attachments, consistent emotional warmth, predictable responses, maintain contact with other family members and significant others.

The dimensions of family and environmental factors:

- **Family History and Functioning** – genetic and psycho-social factors, household composition, history of parent's own childhood, life events, family functioning, sibling relationships, parental strengths and difficulties, absent parents, separated parents relationship.
- **Wider Family** – who does the child feel attached to? Related and non-related persons and wider family, role of relatives and friends, the importance of other people in family network.
- **Housing** – amenities, accessibility, sanitation, cooking facilities, sleeping arrangements, hygiene, and safety.
- **Employment** – who works, pattern of employment, meaning of work to child, impact of work or absence of work on child.
- **Income** – availability, sufficiency, welfare benefits, how resources are used, financial difficulties and the effect on child.
- **Family's Social Integration** – local neighbourhood, community, degree of integration or isolation, peer groups, friendships, social networks.
- **Community Resources** – local facilities and resources, health care, day care, schools, places of worship, transport, shops, leisure activities, standard of resources.

The complex interplay across all three domains should be carefully understood and analysed. The interactions between different factors within the domains are not straightforward. It is important then to gather and record information accurately and systematically. Information should be checked and discussed with parents and children. Differences in perceptions about the information and its relative significance should be recorded. It is important to assess and understand the strengths and difficulties within families and relate these to the vulnerabilities and protective factors in the child's world. The impact of what is happening on the child should be clearly identified (DoH, 2000).

Table 3.2 illustrates a useful resource that was recently devised to incorporate a more positive view of assessment with children and adolescents. Social workers can adapt this for use with parents to help empower them by understanding the detail of the problem and to focus on what needs to change. The strengths and difficulties questionnaire addresses four areas of difficult behaviour: emotional symptoms, conduct problems, hyperactivity, and peer problems (Goodman, 1997). It includes a prosocial behaviour (strengths) dimension to produce a numerical score with descriptions that are easy to recognise. One of its advantages is that professionals and parent/carers can use it to measure change in the child's behaviour before and after intervention. It therefore moves away from some of the more negative, deficit-oriented assessment instruments. Free copies of the questionnaire with background notes are available from *www.youthinmind.net* and further detailed information from www.sdqinfo.com.

Nearly 60,000 children were being looked after by local authorities in England in 2001. Of these children 38,400 were in foster placements and 3,400 were placed for adoption. Since 1995 the numbers of children being looked after have risen year on year (DoH, 2001). There is compelling evidence that children placed in public care by social workers often suffer from a lack of help for their mental health problems and a lack of support to promote their mental health (Mental Health Foundation, 1999; Richardson and Joughin, 2000). This highlights the necessity for patient, accurate, in-depth, and child-focused work in order to arrive at the best solution to the presenting problem. Failure to do so will have serious long-term consequences. Children in care are more likely to have experienced significantly more risk factors, which predispose young people to develop mental health problems that continue into adulthood. A study of the prevalence of mental health problems among young people in the care system in Oxfordshire revealed 67 per cent with significant mental health problems (McCann et al., 1996).

It should be no surprise therefore that the incidence of placement breakdowns in foster care is so high with foster carers often complaining about inadequate support from social workers to help them cope with the most damaged and difficult children (DoH, 1998). The shortage of experienced foster carers, and particularly black foster carers, combined with pressure to move children quickly through the care system hinders thoughtful practice. With all the legal, political, administrative, and procedural pressures impacting on social workers, the temptation is to cut corners at the expense of denying those essential relationships, interpretative and psycho-social skills.

Table 3.2: Strengths and difficulties questionnaire (Goodman, 1997)

	Not true	Somewhat true	Certainly true
Considerate of other peoples feelings			
Restless, overactive, cannot stay still for long			
Often complains of headaches, stomach-aches			
Shares readily with other children			
Often has temper tantrums or hot tempers			
Rather solitary, tends to play alone			
Generally obedient, usually does what adults ask			
Many worries, often seems worried			
Helpful if someone is hurt, upset or feeling ill			
Has at least one good friend			
Constantly fidgeting or squirming			
Often fights with other children or bullies them			
Often unhappy, down-hearted or tearful			
Generally liked by other children			
Easily distracted, concentration wanders			
Nervous or clingy in new situations, easily loses confidence			
Kind to younger children			
Often lies or cheats			
Picked on or bullied by other children			
Often volunteers to help others			
Thinks things out before acting			
Steals from home, school or elsewhere			
Gets on better with adults than other children			
Many fears, easily scared			
Sees tasks through to the end, good attention span			

Key to these is the listening skills which can, with patience, time and supervision, enable the voice of the child to be heard against the background noise of recrimination, blame and anger that can characterise fraught situations. Here, the psycho-social model of practice and supervision can help the social worker bombarded by conflicting narratives and impossible dilemmas, to interrogate their emotional responses in order to bring clarity and a measured response to help negotiate the optimum way forward.

Social workers in this context face the difficult dilemma of the vocabulary and language employed by psychiatric diagnostic criteria, or educational institutions, which can become part of the negative labelling process for these young people. The consequent stigma of mental health is magnified by the already prevailing stigma of social work involvement and being in state care. This runs the danger of further adding to the stress, feelings of isolation, and reproduction of behaviour that reinforces the problem.

Domestic violence itself has traditionally been hard to quantify and tackle effectively because of the hidden nature, and under-reporting of the crime (Hague and Malos, 1993). A review of the literature on the psychological effects on children who witness domestic violence concluded that there is a diversity of findings suggesting that boys do not necessarily imitate externalised aggressive behaviour and girls do not learn to imitate internalised passive behaviour (Kolbo, Blakley and Engelman, 1996). This is important for social workers assessing the impact on these children and considering the possible mental health consequences if non-stereotyped behaviour results.

Social workers have tended in the past to overlook the emotional impact on children of witnessing or becoming involved in domestic violence, focusing on ensuring physical safety of the mother and short term practical support. The evidence suggests a complex picture in terms of the variables likely to influence how individual children suffer mental health consequences (Hester et al., 2000; Mullender et al., 2000; Walker, 2001a). Further research is required to isolate those factors that predispose children similar in age, gender, race and socio-economic status, to widely different reactions.

In terms of the connection between child and adolescent mental health problems and child protection, the revised guidelines for working together facilitated the use of emotional abuse as a joint category of registration (DoH, 1999). Evidence suggests that in the case of emotional abuse the vulnerability of children of sole/primary carers is increased (Glaser et al., 2001). The three particular areas for concern in this area and their inter-related nature are:

- **Harmful parental attributes** – particularly mental ill health, domestic violence and alcohol/drug abuse.
- **Forms of adult ill-treatment** – particularly denigration or rejection.
- **Indicators of child impairment** – particularly unhappiness, underachievement, aggression and school non-attendance.

The indicators of child impairment are, as discussed previously, partly determined by the child's age, gender, temperament and position in the family group. Despite the variety and multiplicity of indicators of impairment or mental health problems, not enough is yet known about the relationship between harmful parental attributes and specific categories of ill-treatment or between ill-treatment and particular emotional or behavioural problems (Glaser et al., 2001). This knowledge could inform better targeting of specific interventions.

Research demonstrates that children placed on the child protection register in the category of emotional abuse were older and had been known to social workers for years. The implications were so serious that there was a higher rate of placements out of home following registration than for other categories. The prognosis for these children was poor therefore emphasising the need for earlier recognition of emotional abuse, better preventive services, improved liaison between staff working with adult harmful attributes and staff working in the area of child mental health, and improved forms of family support.

A major inquiry into child and adolescent mental health concluded that a cultural shift was required which prioritised family support, with a universally acceptable service of non-stigmatising provision. This should be available in schools, GPs, and other accessible venues in order to address the increased trend of mental health problems in children and young people (Mental Health Foundation, 1999). Service-driven models of social work assessment for children and families are the product of a reactive system geared to responding to concerns relating to child protection, developmental harm, or disturbed symptoms within a deficit framework. This leads to a focus on risk assessment that can be experienced by parents as undermining, or psychiatric treatment that constructs the child as suffering an individual disease requiring individual treatment.

Multi-faceted assessment

The literature on assessment in child and adolescent mental health and current Department of Health guidance are nevertheless gradually improving to emphasise multi-faceted assessment. However, they are still influenced by Western psychiatric classifications located in a medico-biological model, and psychotherapeutic concepts narrowly focused on attachment theory (DoH, 1999; Baradon et al., 1999). There is less emphasis on psycho-social factors, including the effects of poverty, racism, unemployment and poor housing. There is evidence of some fresh thinking in this area where attempts to offer a more sophisticated model of assessment are being made stressing the interactive quality of assessment variables and the need for enhanced interpretative and planning skills (Middleton, 1997; Milner and O'Byrne, 1998).

The emphasis is on the need for analysing and weighing the information generated during the assessment process ensuring this is underpinned by partnership practice. A number of themes emerge from the research literature that helps to consider how to achieve this in the context of family and children's difficulties. These include the importance of multi-factorial causal explanations and the contribution of structural variables to childhood problems articulated by several authors (Sutton, 1999; Cole et al., 1995; Rutter et al., 1994). Understanding assessment as a *process* rather than a single *event* will help create the appropriate atmosphere with children and their carers, who require patience and a calm, measured stance from the assessing social worker.

Assessment is also thought of as a one-way process. It is something done by social workers to others or it involves the gathering of information from those apparently familiar with the child or adolescent of concern. Social workers can benefit from appreciating the *interactive* nature of the assessment process. In other words the very nature of assessment will affect that which is being assessed. Simply engaging with a child in some basic drawing or play activity to gain an understanding of them can begin to change the child's behaviour. Interpretation of the child's emotional and behavioural state therefore needs to take account of the potential impact of the assessment process.

The importance of variation in perception of children's behaviour depending on the theoretical model used, and the evidence on assessment methodology is crucial in determining the course and type of support offered. The interplay of these factors and the beneficial effects of developing a synthesis of models of intervention suggest precise targeted responses to particular children's difficulties combined with an expansive approach addressing social issues affecting children and families (Hill, 1999). The different way children's behaviour is understood by the child, the parent or carer and the professionals who encounter the child are important to acknowledge and incorporate in any care plan or supportive intervention. Differences in perception can therefore be seen as explanatory potential rather than implicitly conflictual.

Social workers have the opportunity to employ communication and relationship skills in direct family support work which they traditionally find rewarding and which service users find more acceptable than intrusive, investigative risk assessment. The social work role in multi-agency assessment and planning becomes significant in this context where several perceptions can be expressed, based on diverse evidence and different levels of professional anxiety. Social workers managing these processes with individuals or groups in planning meetings, case conferences or case reviews require advanced negotiation and decision-making skills.

Early warning signs

One of the necessary skills is in determining whether the problems being described about a child or young person by others are transitory and indicative of a stressful developmental transition, or whether the behaviour is long lasting and becoming entrenched. The former can pass after adaptation leaving behind an area of sensitivity, whereas the latter requires attention before establishing a mental health problem echoing throughout adulthood. The next chapter examines ways in which the assessing social worker can continue to develop this skill in the context of culturally competent practice. Meanwhile, the following early characteristics have been found to exist frequently in children and young people who can develop mental health problems (Donnellan, 2000):

Troubling feelings:
- sad and hopeless without good reason
- angry a lot of the time and overreacts to small challenges
- worthless or guilty
- anxious or worried more than most other children
- constant concern about physical problems or appearance
- unexplained fears

Sudden changes:
- loses interest in long term hobby
- unexplained change in eating or sleeping habits
- wants to be alone most of the time
- deterioration in school performance
- excessive daydreaming

Problematic behaviour:
- poor concentration
- persistent nightmares
- obsessional behaviour
- alcohol or drug misuse
- self induced vomiting after eating
- persistent diet and weight loss
- harming others and delinquency

Summary of key points

A psycho-social perspective enables social workers to appreciate the external context of the child and family's experience, combined with internal individual factors that may be affecting the child or young person's mental health. Assessment of child and adolescent mental health problems needs to consider but not get bogged down in, the debate between nature/nurture influences.

A developmental perspective can aid assessment by placing the child or young person in a framework that recognises the on-going human process, rather than trying to describe a static situation. Social work interviewing skills are crucial to the success of an assessment interview with a child or young person. Planning, setting boundaries, being curious and open-minded, as well as reflecting empathy and intuition will pay dividends.

Risk and resilience factors are important to use to help focus on the detail of general assessment information, but they are not definitive instruments. Trying to fit children and adolescents into pre-fixed categories is at best oppressive and at worst dangerous. The skill is in using the theoretical resources to inform and guide an individualised, person-centred assessment.

Assessment guidelines for children in need are a comprehensive resource for social workers that reflect a psycho-social developmental perspective. Used flexibly this can assist in CAMH assessment especially if time is spent analysing the interplay between the three elements of child, parent, and environment. The results can then help determine the focus of future intervention and inter-agency planning to achieve this.

CHAPTER 4

Culturally Competent Practice

Introduction

After the Second World War the needs of developed countries such as Britain required labour to drive the engine of economic recovery. The Caribbean islands provided such a cheap source of labour and black people were encouraged to come to Britain to settle and work in the new public authorities established in the post war construction of the Welfare State. In the past thirty years ethnic wars rooted in the aftermath of colonialism and West European imperialism have prompted a massive movement of people across continents seeking asylum from areas of conflict and persecution. Europe, which had been a continent of emigration for hundreds of years, has now become a continent of immigration.

The shifting population demographics of the United States of America indicate that ethnic minority children will become the majority of those under age eighteen within the next fifty years. In Britain, and in other European countries, in some areas ethnic minority families make up a greater proportion of the population. Globalisation, European economic and political convergence, and the relaxation of boundaries between countries are enabling the displacement of asylum seeking and refugee families.

These factors, combined with the widening gap between rich and poor countries, are all contributing to the accelerating historical trends of migration and immigration leading to the widening and deepening of the multi-cultural tapestry of complex, modern, diverse Western societies. Research has highlighted the inequitable, oppressive, and poor quality services available for ethnic minority families in these societies (Cole et al., 1995; Bhui, 1997; Bhui and Olajide, 1999; Fernando, 2002). It is crucial therefore, that the organisation and training of all professionals working in child and adolescent mental health services – especially social workers – is culturally competent.

Cultural competence has been defined as a set of congruent attitudes, behaviours, and policies that are part of an agency, system or professional group, and that enable these groups to work effectively in cross-cultural situations. For individual practitioners to achieve competence they must be aware of their own culture, refrain from judging differences as necessarily deviant and understand the dynamics of working class cultures. They must develop a base of knowledge about the child's culture, and adapt their skills to fit the child or young person's cultural context (Cross et al., 1989).

The discipline of psychiatry, which dominates child and adolescent mental health provision, has resisted any significant influence by systems of culture that were not specifically European. The development of psychiatry and theories of human growth and development constructed in the 18th and 19th centuries were based on white ethnocentric beliefs and assumptions about normality. The Western model of illness regards the mind as distinct from the body and defines mental illness or mental health according to negative, deficit characteristics as noted in Chapter 2. In non-western cultures such as Chinese, Indian and African, mental health is often perceived as a harmonious balance between a person's internal and external influences. Thus a person is intrinsically linked to their environment and vice versa.

The Western model of mental illness ignores the religious or spiritual aspects of the culture in which it is based. However, Eastern, African and Native American cultures tend to integrate them (Fernando, 2002). Spirituality and religion as topics in general do not feature often in the social work literature, yet they can be critical components of a child and young person's well being offering a source of strength, and hope in trying circumstances. Children for whom family and faith backgrounds are inseparable may need encouragement to feel comfortable in multi-faith settings. Social workers need to address this dimension as part of the constellation of factors affecting black children and adolescents, bearing in mind the positive and sometimes negative impact spiritual or religious beliefs might have on their mental health. Children communicate about feelings and experiences more easily through responses to stories. Direct social work that allows them to use their imaginations and access their own spirituality through stories can be liberating.

In a postcolonial world, the rights and expectations of indigenous people to reparation and how they are perceived are important issues in the context of achieving culturally competent practice. The disparities between developed and developing economies under the influence of globalisation are becoming more pronounced, incorporating new forms of cultural domination. The concept of cultural and social injustice can be illustrated thus (Powell, 2001):

- **Cultural domination** – some people are excluded because they are subjected to ways of interpreting or communicating which originate from a culture which is not their own, and which may be alien or hostile to them.
- **Non-recognition** – some people are excluded because they are effectively rendered invisible by the dominant cultural practices.
- **Cultural disrespect** – some people are excluded because they are routinely devalued by the stereotyping of public representations or everyday interactions within the dominant cultural context.

The legislative and policy context

Issues of citizenship and nationality, race and immigration provide the overarching context within legislation and public policy which sets the scene for racist and oppressive practice to go unchecked. The British Nationality Act (HMSO, 1948) provided legal rights to immigration which have served as a focal point for a continuing racialised debate about the numbers of black immigrants and refugee/asylum seekers and the perceived social problems subsequently caused (Solomos, 1989). The Race Relations (Amendment) Act (HMSO, 2000) came into force in 2001 extending the scope of the Race Relations Act (HMSO, 1976). The new Act strengthens the law in two ways that are significant to social work practice:

- **It extends protection against racial discrimination by public authorities.**
- **It places a new, enforceable positive duty on public authorities.**

Like the Human Rights Act (UN, 1998), the new Act defines a public authority very widely. Anyone whose work involves functions of a public nature must not discriminate on racial grounds while carrying out those functions. The most important aspect of the new Act in the long term will be the new positive duty on local authorities because it gives statutory force to the imperative of tackling institutional racism. The new general duty replaces section 71 of the Race Relations Act 1976 with a tougher requirement on public authorities to eliminate unlawful discrimination and promote equality of opportunity and good race relations in carrying out their functions.

At the 1991 census just over 3 million (5.5 per cent) of the 55 million people in Britain did not classify themselves as white. Half are South Asian (that is of Indian, Pakistani, and Bangladeshi descent) and 30 per cent are black. The rich diversity of Britain's minority populations is illustrated in Table 4.1 but importantly, nearly half of Britain's non-white population had been born in Britain, with three quarters of these registered British citizens. The overwhelming majority of non-white children under 16 were born in Britain.

The Nationality, Immigration and Asylum Bill (HMSO, 2002) is the fourth piece of primary legislation attempting to reform the asylum system in 10 years. Previous measures related to dispersal and support measures and were widely regarded as harmful to children's health because they resulted in sub-standard accommodation, isolation, discrimination and poverty (Dennis and Smith, 2002; JCWI, 2002). The new Law proposes the establishment of accommodation centres housing about 3,000 people in rural areas. Protection of children in such places will be difficult due to the high turnover of residents, while these children will be impeded from opportunities to integrate and feel part of society.

In addition, the new Law proposes denying asylum-seeking children the right to be educated in mainstream local schools. Such segregation could contravene the Human Rights Act 1998 and the UN Convention on the Rights of the Child (UN, 1989) because this is not in the best interests of the child and will very likely harm their development and mental health. Children, who have suffered extreme

Table 4.1: People born outside Great Britain and resident here, by countries of birth,1991 (Owen, 1992–1995)

Countries of birth	No. resident in Britain	% of Britain's population
Northern Ireland	245,000	0.45
Irish republic	592,000	1.08
Germany	216,000	0.39
Italy	91,000	0.17
France	53,000	0.10
Other EC	133,900	0.24
Scandinavia and EFTA	58,300	0.11
E. Europe and former USSR	142,900	0.26
Cyprus	78,000	0.14
Rest of Near and Middle East	58,300	0.11
Aust, NZ and Canada	177,400	0.32
New Commonwealth	1,688,400	3.08
Jamaica	142,000	0.26
Rest of Caribbean	122,600	0.22
India	409,000	0.75
Pakistan	234,000	0.43
Bangladesh	105,000	0.19
Rest of South Asia	39,500	0.07
South East Asia	150,400	0.27
East Africa	220,600	0.40
West and Southern Africa	110,700	0.20
Rest of the World	566,200	1.03
Asia	231,000	0.42
North Africa	44,600	0.08
South Africa	68,000	0.12
Rest of Africa	34,300	0.06
USA	143,000	0.26
Rest of Americas	42,000	0.08
Total born outside GB	3,991,000	7.27

trauma, anxiety and hardship, need to feel safe, included and part of their community with their peers in order to begin to thrive and rebuild their fragile mental health. There are doubts that the quality of education offered in accommodation centres would properly meet even basic standards of pedagogic practice.

The proposals on marriage and family visits in the Law are another potential source of anxiety and psychological harm to children and young people. The subject of arranged marriage combines further attempts to restrict entry from abroad with a barely disguised racist attack on cultural practices in some black communities. A two-year probationary period for marriages is proposed in order to test the integrity of individuals who enter into marriages abroad with non-British citizens. The effect will be to increase the number of children confronting the prospect of separation from one parent because of doubts raised about whether their parents' marriage will subsist indefinitely.

Understanding black and ethnic minority families

Institutionalised racism, failure of welfare services to listen to and respond to the concerns of black communities, stereotypical beliefs about black families, and barriers to access, all inhibit equal opportunity for black children with mental health problems to receive help. Social workers attuned to anti discriminatory values will be at an advantage over other professionals working in this area but they need to avoid complacency and collusion with covert institutional and personal racism. While it is important to avoid stereotypes of different black and ethnic minority families it is as important to understand that they each share in common the painful experiences as a consequence of endemic prejudice in a racist society.

Anti-racist action and the theoretical basis underpinning it has been subjected to political assault over the years. This climate has permitted oppressive practices to become embedded in social and health care services with the acquiescence of a managerialist culture itself oppressed by government financial and policy strictures. The evidence demonstrating the prevention of initial and equal access and the inappropriateness of service provision has consistently been highlighted (Ely and Denney, 1987; Atkin and Rollings, 1993; DoH, 2000). However, there is not enough evidence that certain service characteristics are as relevant in their contribution to effectiveness in improving access as is frequently claimed.

Cultural or ethnic congruence between service users and staff is perceived as a good strategy to improve service acceptability and accessibility. Yet there is no substantive body of evidence to support this, even though it instinctively feels right. An evaluative approach such as that described by Courtney et al. (1996) suggests that differences in service provision outcomes should be assessed using robust evaluation designs. This is preferable rather than simply trying to recruit black staff en masse and assume service improvement will follow. Such an approach based on actual evidence can be employed to distinguish what works best for which black children and families, avoiding a colour-blind approach which evades the issue by claiming equal access to all regardless of race or cultural differences, or misguided attempts to provide culturally-sensitive but ineffective support.

Refugee and asylum seeking families experience additional stresses making them and their children highly vulnerable to mental health problems. They face relentless discrimination, racism, persecution, and suspicion from host countries that in many cases treat them as illegal immigrants, criminalising their attempts at survival. Studies of the psychological effects of homelessness on children are useful in measuring the potential impact on asylum seeking families housed in temporary accommodation (Heath, 1994; Amery, Tomkins and Victor, 1995; Vostanis, 1999). They demonstrate that these families constitute a high-risk group for the development of mental health problems and disorders. The stress caused by events precipitating their homelessness, combined with the trauma of displacement can undermine normal protective and resilience factors in both parents and children.

The disproportionate presence of black communities in areas of high social need means that specific economic and environmental factors should be identified when assessing families, and the mental health needs of their children, rather than relying on generalised ethnic differences (Shah, 1994). While working class families also receive inappropriate or ineffective services, the evidence that black children are less likely to access help, places them at a further disadvantage (Smaje,1994; Dominelli, 1998). The characteristics of a service for black children and adolescents with mental health problems which aspires to better accessibility can be described as composing of three elements:

- **Consultation** – with individual black families and their communities is required to ensure service provision meets their needs and to identify gaps in services. A pro-active community-oriented practice offers a practical and effective way of achieving this.
- **Information** – needs to be provided about rights and responsibilities in the context of childcare and mental health legislation. Jargon-free material should be accessible in different formats and languages about child and adolescent mental health needs.
- **Competence** – staff competence in child and adolescent mental health is not enough if this is not matched with demonstrable knowledge and skills required to practice in an ethnically diverse society.

Social workers need to distinguish between offering *equal* standards of service to black families and a service that is the *same.* The notion that staff are treating all service users equally could easily end up with them treating black families the same, which is inappropriate. Another potential area for confusion is the concept of ethnic record keeping and the distinction with ethnic monitoring. Record keeping on its own is only a superficial attempt at promoting equality of access to a service. Ethnic monitoring is about using the information in a systematic way to differentiate the subtle characteristics of diverse communities and the evaluation and review of services provided for them (Caesar et al., 1994).

The prevalence of adult mental health problems is estimated at 10 per cent, with disproportionately higher rates among black and ethnic minority families. The diagnosis of schizophrenia among black men, and that of depression and suicide in Asian women are two areas where it is acknowledged that cultural factors combined with inadequate service provision for their particular needs, are combining to severely disadvantage these particular groups (Bhugra and Bahl, 1999). A history of childhood mental health problems is strongly indicated in the risk factors for developing adult mental health problems. It is imperative therefore that the needs of black and ethnic minority children vulnerable to mental health problems are addressed early in order to prevent later problems and the subsequent damage they can cause to the individual, their family, and the environment.

The aim of culturally appropriate practice is to exclude the risk of misinterpretation or underplaying significant emotional and behavioural characteristics. In Britain the suicide rate among young men between the ages of 15 and 19 has more than doubled in the last 30 years. Worryingly, research has shown that in 60 per cent of these cases the young person had been demonstrating signs of emotional or behavioural difficulties for months before (McConville, 2001). The evidence demonstrates that black children are more likely to be perceived as physically aggressive in classrooms, and subsequently subject to racist stereotyping. When these young people react against this discrimination, they inadvertently feed the self-fulfilling prophecies of teachers who perceive them in the same way, and thus perpetuate a negative interactive cycle. Social workers involved in such cases need to bring an extra and more socially informed perspective to inter-agency discussions concerning aggressive behaviour in black youth.

Equally, an understanding of the reluctance and resistance of parents to consider a mental health explanation for their child's behaviour or emotional state is particularly important when considering how to engage black and ethnic minority parents or carers in the process of support. Different cultural explanations based on physical or spiritual causation may need to be acknowledged, as well as fears of additional labelling marking out their children for further racist abuse. Denial, self-blame and guilt are powerful feelings generated at times of distress and bewilderment – a psycho-social perspective can help untangle these and enable parents or carers to move forward. Rather than seek to question and challenge parental explanations, social workers need to use listening and communications skills to affirm and contain parents' worries. This will give them the space in which to discuss and consider the way forward rather than dispute diagnostic labels or obscure theories.

Parents coping strategies are easily diminished at times of crisis or after prolonged periods of difficulty, the effects of which can then cascade through the family system disrupting the self-regulatory patterns of comfort and support usually available at times of stress. Apart from homeless refugee and asylum seeking families, black and other ethnic minority families will at times need to reside in temporary accommodation or refuges, sometimes at very short notice.

The circumstances could be domestic violence, child protection, marital/partner relationship breakdown or an adult mental health crisis. Staff working in Housing Services in the responsible authority may not be attuned to the emotional needs of such families, concentrating on the provision of basic necessities and support services.

Social workers involved need to take a broad holistic and psycho-social approach to their intervention and not overlook the need for careful assessment of mental health problems developing in children, whilst naturally responding to the practical needs of the families. If these are not tackled promptly, because of other apparent priorities and the difficulties in accessing appropriate specialist help, these children may go on to develop serious and persistent difficulties which are harder, and more costly to resolve in the long term.

The mental health needs of culturally diverse children

The evidence for the need to distinguish the different mental health needs of all children in a culturally diverse society and protect them from racist abuse is strong (Barter, 1999; Blackwell and Melzak, 2000; Chand, 2000; Weaver and Burns, 2001; Stanley, 2001). For example, refugee and asylum seeking children, some unaccompanied, many affected by extreme circumstances, might include those witnessing murder of parents or kin. They will also have experienced dislocation from school and community, severing of important friendships and extended family support, loss of home, and prolonged insecurity. These experiences will likely trigger symptoms consistent with post traumatic stress syndrome. This is manifested in a variety of ways including: shock, grief, depression, anxiety, hyperactivity, self harming behaviour, anger, aggressive behaviour, fear, and guilt. Each individual child or adolescent will react differently according to variables such as:

- The context of their departure from the home country.
- The family cohesion and coping capacity.
- The child's own personality and predisposing psychological constitution.
- Proximity to extreme acts of murder or violence.
- The child's developmental stage and history of transition.

A number of studies compared levels of stress in adolescents and family functioning across different national boundaries including Canada, United States, Britain, Malaysia, India, Hong Kong and the Philippines (Bagley and Mallick, 1995; Bochner, 1994; Gibson-Cline, 1996; Watkins and Gerong, 1997; Martin, Rozanes, Pearce and Allison, 1995). A meta-analysis of these studies tested the hypothesis that while subjectively perceived levels of stress can vary significantly between cultures, the underlying causes of personal distress could be relatively similar between cultures (Bagley and Mallick, 2000). This is useful information to consider when trying to practice in culturally competent ways, that avoid racist stereotyping.

The differences in reported prevalence rates of mental health problems in various countries may reflect different classification systems, rather than real differences. Therefore, family dysfunction as perceived by the child or adolescent will, with other perceived stressors, be a statistically significant predictor of various kinds of problem behaviours and emotional states in all ethnic groups. The conclusion is that there is a measurable, culturally universal, aspect of the relations of adolescents to family and other stress in terms of emotional and behavioural problems, and impaired self-esteem. However, a causal pattern from stress to mental health problems cannot be demonstrated beyond reasonable doubt.

The strongest evidence for prediction of mental health problems in children and adolescents across cultures, is that for general family stress (Bagley and Mallick, 2000). Looked at more closely this includes the effects of physical, sexual, and emotional abuse in the context of a climate of persistent negative family interactions. These findings are supported by other studies, which seek to illuminate and distinguish the particular factors influencing those children likely to develop mental health problems (Bagley and Young, 1998; Kashani and Allan, 1998; Vincent and Jouriles, 2000). Social workers seeking to intervene effectively have to carefully consider the various ways potential mental health problems are thought about, understood, and communicated in every family, in every culture.

It is argued that children do not have one essential identity, but switch identities in different situations and, subject to a diversity of cultural influences, can produce new identities (Ackroyd and Pilkington, 1999). Social workers employing anti-racist and anti-discriminatory principles may simplistically try to reinforce apparent cultural norms that are not applicable, or explain disturbed behaviour in terms of cultural features, which are irrelevant. This underlines the importance of understanding the culture within the culture-in other words finding out what are the individual and family norms, preferences, styles, habits and patterns of relationships that make that family what it is in the particular context of social work involvement.

For example there is an assumption that Asian families are close-knit with extended family relationships often living together in multi-generational households. This is a stereotype and may apply to a lot of Asian families but the danger is in applying the stereotype unthinkingly instead of using it to test a hypothesis about the particular family being helped. In many circumstances taking into account the concept of extended family relationships in close proximity can aid assessment of emerging mental health problems in an Asian child or young person. But assuming this is always a sign of family strength and harmonious supportive relationships is risking missing obscure destructive dynamics that may be contributing to the child's mental health problems. These factors are beginning to emerge as some Asian youth struggle to balance loyalty to their history and culture with the different values and pressures in their environment (Qureshi et al., 2000; Fernando, 2002).

There is a fine balance between normalising behaviour attributed to various causal factors, and moving too quickly to apply or support a psychiatric diagnosis inappropriately. Each way of conceptualising the presenting problem has implications for the short and long term outcomes of social work assessment and intervention. A failure to recognise and acknowledge significant mental health problems could be just as damaging to the young person and others involved with them, as could seeking to explain their behaviour with a definitive psychiatric diagnosis. For some young people it could be a relief to have an explanation for feelings and behaviour that they find hard to make sense of, whereas for others it could exacerbate feelings of blame, guilt and self-loathing. The enduring social stigma of mental health problems in addition to racist experiences provides an overall context for these feelings to be repressed, displaced, or acted out.

Black and other ethnic minority children are disproportionately represented in the public care system. They have often been developmentally delayed, may have learning disabilities, have difficulty with communication, experience failure at school, and are at risk of beginning to establish persistent delinquent behaviours. Like many other children in the care system they face considerable hardship, which is built upon a history of failure, missed opportunity and psychological trauma. Their life opportunities and prospects are poor with a high risk of future psycho-social problems. Social workers in residential care or in looked after/continuing care teams need a perspective that fully embraces anti-racist practice combined with an appreciation of the mental health needs of this disadvantaged group of children.

Very little of the research on the mental health consequences of black and other ethnic minority children witnessing domestic violence has examined the impact race and racism might have on these children. It has been suggested that the societal context of racism provide these children with a sense of refuge inside their own home. However, when violence occurs inside their home as well, this can have profound effects on their sense of security and vulnerability, triggering acute anxiety-related symptoms (Imam, 1994). For these children there is no hiding place. Some of the negative impacts on black children are likely to be exacerbated by additional threats of abduction abroad, or by being asked inappropriately to act as interpreters or translators in situations where their welfare is at stake.

Globalisation and emancipation

The term globalisation has begun to feature in the social work literature reflecting profound shifts in the economic and social patterns of relationships between the richer industrialised countries and the poorer developing countries. It involves closer international economic integration prompted by the needs of capitalism, but also has demographic, social, cultural and psychological dimensions (Midgley, 2001). Consistent with the link between the social context of child and adolescent mental health problems, it is therefore important to consider the global context in terms of the challenges for building culturally competent practice.

Critics of globalisation argue that its impact is to maintain unequal power relationships between the richer and poorer countries so that patterns of wealth and consumer consumption in Europe and North America can be sustained. This involves the exploitation of labour and other resources in poorer countries thereby preventing them achieving a diverse and equitable economic and social structure within which health and social welfare programmes can develop. In Britain the consequences of globalisation are being noticed in the way traditional social care systems are taking on the characteristics of business ethics and commercialism (Dominelli, 1999; Mishra, 1999). One of the side effects of this process is the standardisation and conformity required for consumer consumption patterns in order to maximise profit. The consequence is the steady and inexorable erosion of traditional markers of indigenous cultural identity combined with the elevation of global branding.

This critique of the latest phase of capitalist development echoes earlier concerns about the impact on economic growth and subsequent erosion of traditional government policies of full employment and social welfare (Corrigan and Leonard, 1978; Bailey and Brake, 1980). A failure to fully develop social welfare services, or to have them subjected to the gyrations of speculative global financial markets, invariably corrodes the quality and the depth of services designed to reach children and families in personal and culturally appropriate ways. This means that services are pared to the minimum, oriented towards crisis intervention and designed in the narrowest terms to conform to inflexible eligibility criteria that limit access. These features are inconsistent with culturally competent practice that aims to spread accessibility, improve acceptability and enrich social worker's creative potential to respond to a diverse society.

Dilemmas in trends towards cultural competence have been highlighted by reference to the practice of forced/arranged marriages and dowry, genital mutilation of children, and harsh physical punishments condoned by some societies (Midgley, 2001). These practices can be used to counter the argument for respecting ethnic and cultural diversity and support the notion of universal social work values as the basis for competent practice. Ethnic rivalries and the pride in national identity on which they are based also sit uneasily with culturally competent aspirations of international collaboration and mutual understanding.

However, rather than seek answers to these difficult issues in an introspective way, this emphasises the need for social workers and their professional representatives to reach out to the international social work community with service users, to continue to debate, discuss and strive for ways to discover solutions. In the area of child and adolescent mental health social workers need to understand the impact such practices and the beliefs on which they are based are having on the mental health and emotional development of those adults promoting them and the children and young people experiencing them.

Cultural competence has been defined as developing skills in assessing the cultural climate of an organisation and being able to practice in a strategic manner within it. It has also been broadened to include *any* context in which social workers practice in order to permit effective direct work at many levels (Baldwin, 2000; Fook, 2002). Whether at the strategic organisational level or the direct interpersonal level social workers can actively resist those pressures to conformity and routinised practice that in often discreet and inconspicuous ways can undermine efforts to practise in culturally competent ways. The requirements of social justice demand vigilance and creativity in order to contribute towards an emancipatory practice that can liberate both social workers and service users from prescribed practice orthodoxies. Such practice is the antithesis of stereotyped, one-dimensional thinking and is characterised by (Leonard, 1994):

- A commitment to standing alongside oppressed and impoverished populations.
- The importance of dialogic relations between workers and service users.
- Orientation towards the transformation of processes and structures that perpetuate domination and exploitation.

These characteristics are in harmony with culturally competent practice. They do not imply that social workers should reject statutory practice for the voluntary sector, child care for community work, or psychodyamic theories for advocacy. These simplistic oppositional devices do not help social workers manage the complexities and dilemmas in seeking different practice orientations (Healy, 2002). The possibilities for creative practice within organisational constraints are there. They may be limited and subjected to pressures of time but in the personal relationship with service users and particularly children and adolescents with mental health problems, the rewards are unquantifiable for both worker and client. Even introducing a small change in practice can have a much larger disproportionate and beneficial impact.

Components of culturally competent practice

One of the defining features of social work practice is the ability to work closely with other professionals and communities, often in a co-ordinating role or as a client advocate. This role in the context of work with child and adolescent mental health problems is crucial at various points of the assessment and intervention process to ensure culturally competent practice (Canino and Spurlock, 2000; Madge, 2001). Cultural competence can be defined as a set of knowledge-based and interpersonal skills that allow individuals to understand, appreciate and work with individuals of cultures, from other than their own. Five components have been identified comprising culturally competent care (Kim, 1995):

- Awareness and acceptance of cultural differences.
- Capacity for cultural self-awareness.
- Understanding the dynamics of difference.
- Developing basic knowledge about the child's culture.
- Adapting practice skills to fit the cultural context of the child and family.

These are consistent with other work which critique the historical development of cross-cultural services and offer a model of service organisation and development designed to meet the needs of ethnic minority families (Moffic and Kinzie, 1996; Bhugra, 1999; Bhugra and Bahl, 1999). Ethnocentric and particularly Eurocentric, explanations of emotional and psycho-social development are not inclusive enough to understand the developments of diverse ethnic minority children. Failure to understand the cultural background of children and adolescents and their families can lead to unhelpful assessments, non-compliance, poor use of services, and alienation of the child and family from the welfare system (Dominelli, 1988).

Social workers using an anti-discriminatory, empowerment model of psycho-social practice are ideally placed to work with other professionals in multi-disciplinary contexts to enable the team to maintain a focus on culturally competent practice. The increased demands for help from parents and children themselves suffering the effects of mental health problems have prompted policy initiatives to invest in and reconfigure child and adolescent mental health service provision. The aim is to make them more accessible and acceptable to all cultures (House of Commons, 1997; Davis et al., 1997; Mental Health Foundation, 1999).

There is evidence that inter-agency training models improve co-ordination of effort between different professionals especially in the important area of primary care and early intervention (Firth et al., 1999; Walker, 2001b; Sebuliba and Vostanis, 2001). Social work has traditionally valued its distinctive role in human welfare provision, spanning the gap between the psychological and social interpretations of human growth and development. The distinguishing features of professional social work, in comparison with other mental health professions, are:

- The explicit value commitments to the service users right to respect and self-determination.
- Addressing the linkage between psychological and social problems of living.
- Taking account of the impact structural racism and discrimination are having.

Inspection of services for black children and their families shows that despite the rhetoric of anti-racist and anti-oppressive social work practice, assessments and care planning are generally inadequate (SSI, 2000). Assessments are often partial and rarely cover parental capacity, the child's needs, and environmental

issues. There is little evidence that care planning takes a lifelong view –
highlighting the failure to recruit black foster carers or understanding the changing
characteristics of this group of children. The guidance suggests:

- Ensuring that services and staffing are monitored by ethnicity to ensure they
  are provided appropriately and equally.
- Involving ethnic minorities in planning and reviewing services.
- Training in anti-racist and anti-discriminatory practice.
- Investigating and monitoring complaints of racial discrimination or
  harassment.
- Explicit policies are in place for working with black families.

Social workers skills in facilitating service user empowerment particularly with
children and adolescent mental health problems are indicated in any vision of the
future shape of service provision (Walker, 2001c). Community social work and
group work are also required to enable families and young people to support each
other and raise collective awareness of shared issues. Investigation of indigenous
healing practices and beliefs provide a rich source of information to utilise in the
helping process. Advocacy skills, in which young people are encouraged to be
supported and represented by advocates of their choice, would help contribute to
influencing current service provision (Ramon, 1999).

The notion that social workers should respect diversity, build on an ethnic
group's strengths, and provide for individual and social change, is not new
(Pentini and Lorenz, 1996). Yet there is a considerable gap in the literature on
social work effectiveness in general, and specifically working with black and ethnic
minority clients. Reviews of social work practice highlight the need for more
rigorous evaluation of what works with which clients in what circumstances with
what methods (Russell, 1990; Thompson, 1995; Shaw, 1996; Cheetham, 1997).
Translating research findings into practice in the context of child and adolescent
mental health services social work can contribute to a more holistic response to
the needs of every child and family that requires it. This can help towards offering
black citizens an equal opportunity to take their rightful place in society and benefit
from its resources.

Culturally competent practice demands that social workers above all do not
avoid the challenge of developing a perspective on child development that
recognises the plurality of pathways to maturity within that perspective. In other
words it is not good enough to rely on a limited, partial understanding of child
development to be applied universally as a measure against which to judge a
child's emotional and psychological progress. The influence of North American
and Eurocentric child psychology literature and theories is extending beyond
those societies from which dominant discourses have been generated. Child
development experts have tailored professional guidance in developing countries
to explicitly assimilate western child development theory into Third World

contexts. Industrialising countries with formerly agricultural histories have a rich reservoir of cultural and familial practices to draw from to inform their understanding of their children's emotional and behavioural development.

Many traditional beliefs and practices are under pressure nowadays under the inexorable momentum of economic and cultural globalisation forcing parents to change attitudes, values, habits and child rearing practices. The consequences for family stability and child and adolescent mental health are traumatic (James and Prout, 1997). Use of the Assessment framework described in the last chapter requires that child and family differences must be approached with knowledge and sensitivity in a non-judgemental way. The danger is that fear, ignorance, and institutional and personal racism can result in a lack of accuracy and balance in analysing a child or young person's needs. Social workers need to avoid:

- Using one set of cultural assumptions and stereotypes to understand the child and family circumstances.
- Insensitivity to racial and cultural variations within groups and between individuals.
- Making unreasoned assumptions without evidence.
- Failing to take account of the barriers which prevent the social integration of black families.
- Attaching meaning to information without confirming the interpretation with the child and family members.

The key principles that underpin the holistic approach of anti-oppressive social work have been summarised by Dominelli (2002):

- **Social Justice** – promotes equality in matters of power and resource distribution and ensures that a person is treated with dignity and respect.
- **Rights and Citizenship** – locates an individual or group within a set of social relationships in which they have access to and receive social and material resources as inalienable entitlements when needed.
- **Solidarity** – embraces the realisation of the value of supporting others through the formation of mutual links of collaboration and support networks.
- **Reciprocity and Interdependence** – acknowledges both giving and receiving when interacting with others to obtain assistance and involves the realisation that no person or group is sufficient unto themselves.

Social workers have a significant role to play in all four Tiers of CAMHS provision as both generic children and family workers or in more specialised child mental health settings to intervene effectively. At the generic level, they can work in multi-disciplinary ways as part of inter-agency groups co-ordinating efforts to support the child and family through temporary or moderate difficulties. This is a crucial and under-researched area of practice where vital early intervention and preventive work can be undertaken but which does not register in quantifiable ways amenable to evaluative inquiry. It is often brief, low profile, fragmented, discrete elements of wider activity, which combined at the appropriate time, can provide just enough help to contain and deflect future problems. In more specialised settings social workers can benefit from in-service post qualifying training which traditionally means family therapy or psychotherapy training both of which to be completed to advance levels are costly and time-consuming. Wherever they work, and in whatever practice orientation, social workers task is to maintain a critical but constructive perspective on their agency's treatment of black and ethnic minority children and young people.

Voluntary projects and family support services organised by charities and church groups attempt to meet sometimes complex needs, on few resources and continual uncertainty over future funding. Assessment and interpretation of behaviour through the spectrum of child developmental milestones that are culturally adapted are required to improve the recognition of potential mental health problems in black children and refer on to specialist resources if necessary. The full range of intellectual and therapeutic resources available to social workers is needed to begin the process of assessment and intervention in harmony with appropriate multi-agency co-operation and participation. Often in these circumstances the resource that can make a big difference to whether an emerging problem becomes a larger and entrenched problem is the availability of consultation or supervision. This subject will be considered further in the next chapter, which offers theoretical and practical resources to enhance social work intervention in child and adolescent mental health practice.

Summary of key points

Historical trends in migration and immigration prompted by ethnic conflict, globalisation and European economic and political convergence, are all leading to the widening and deepening of the multi-cultural tapestry of diversity in Western societies. However, inequitable, discriminatory and racist services are still offered to black and other ethnic minority children and families.

The legislative and policy context in the United Kingdom sets the scene for institutional and personal racism to be condoned especially in relation to refugee and asylum seeking children who are among the most disadvantaged group with mental health problems. Social workers need to avoid colluding with discriminatory practices and maintain an anti-racist perspective that challenges crude stereotyping and values diversity.

A pro-active community-oriented practice that engages with black and other ethnic minority groups needs to ensure meaningful consultation takes place, appropriate information about child and adolescent mental health is provided, and staff are able to practice in culturally competent ways. This means avoiding misinterpretation or underplaying significant characteristics.

Social workers need to strive to find the culture within the culture and to enable the expression of traditional beliefs about children's emotional and psychological development. Investigation of indigenous healing practices, participatory practice and advocacy skills are required to contribute towards culturally competent practice.

CHAPTER 5

Social Work Intervention

Introduction

The role and function of social work intervention in general has been the subject of much discussion throughout the relatively short history of the profession (Giddings, 1898; Richmond, 1922; Titmuss, 1958; Butrym, 1976; Davies, 1981; Barclay, 1982; CCETSW, 1989; Kemshall, 1993; O'Hagan, 1996; Adams et al., 1998). The specific manifestation of that role and function in work with children and young people with mental health problems has tended to receive little attention. This role gets eclipsed between routinised family assessment work and high-risk child protection work, while the trend towards care management underplays therapeutic skills. However in the context of multi-disciplinary working, and methods and models of therapeutic intervention there is evidence of the way a psycho-social model can still be utilised in contemporary social work practice (Brearley, 1995; Copley and Forryan, 1997; Davies, 1997; Howe et al., 1999; Trevithick, 2000).

Every intervention should have a purpose and, as much as possible, that purpose should be identified clearly and openly as part of the agreement established with service users, other key individuals and professionals involved. The seemingly routine task of an assessment interview can be thought of as an intervention in its own right because of the opportunity to gain a greater understanding of people and their situations in a therapeutic way. That is, by using the opportunity to establish a helping relationship as the basis for initiating change, rather than seeing it as an administrative task (Stepney and Ford, 2000; Trevithick, 2000).

The choice of intervention open to social workers in child mental health work is necessarily broad because of the wide variety of psychological and social factors influencing the child or young person being helped. The social work literature itself offers a sometimes bewildering array of methods and models of intervention, apart from the wider psychiatric, psychological, and therapeutic texts available to guide the helping process with individuals, families or groups. Public health, education, social and fiscal policy interventions by local and central government agencies also impact on children's welfare generally and need to be taken into account.

One way of conceptualising this mosaic of influences on children and adolescents and capturing a *meta* view of the panorama of concern is the idea that the variety of influences can be classified into different systems. The notion of a systems approach to formulating interventions was developed thirty years ago and is enshrined in the classic text by Pincus and Minahan which illustrates the variety of systems influencing the service user/client (1973). Within each system of influence are a number of factors, but in the context of this chapter, only those available directly to social workers will be examined in more detail, in order to promote the development of intervention skills.

Before embarking on any one form of intervention though, social workers need to reflect on the ethical questions raised by the choices made and the potential consequences. The legal contexts for intervening in children and young people's lives were considered in Chapter 1 and are relevant to this discussion because of the link with consent and competence to understand choices offered. For example, individual counselling or therapy may succeed in helping a young person to develop a sense of self, but in so doing the experience may alienate them from their family. Family therapy may result in the improvement of a child with emotional difficulties, but in the process of the work siblings may be adversely affected or the parental marriage/partnership exposed as problematic (Sharman, 1997). Even though a social worker may not deliver the work themselves, the act of referring to a specialist resource offering specific help means they are sanctioning a potentially powerful intervention in the lives of the child and their family.

A social worker who feels that a child is bottling up their feelings and needs to learn to express them in counselling may be causing additional stress to the child who is expected within their community or cultural context, to be developing self-control and containment of emotions. A young person who is displaying destructive obsessional behaviour as a means of managing their stress may be given a behavioural or psychodynamic intervention by a social worker depending on the particular preference of that individual worker. However, each intervention comes with its own set of assumptions and potential consequences in terms of generating other stressors. The same intervention could be given to two children with the same problem, but only one of them might benefit. These ethical dilemmas are important to acknowledge and reflect upon before proceeding with any course of action. The crucial point is to ensure the *most* effective intervention is offered for the *appropriate* problem with the *right* child.

Family support

Family Support is probably the most common, and arguably the most important, social work intervention to impact on child mental health problems. It can be defined as self-help or volunteer help with little statutory involvement, or it can mean a continuum of advice, support, and specialist help geared to provide early preventive intervention. The intervention can be directed at individual parents, couples, the child, the whole family, or in groups. It can consist of individual counselling, psychotherapy, group work, advice and information, or the provision of practical help. The place of preventive family support work can be conceptualised using a three-stage model identifying different levels of intervention (Hardiker, 1995):

The primary level offers universally available services that can strengthen family functioning, and spot early signs of mental health problems in children. They are provided by a mix of state and voluntary welfare providers, and parent education services. The secondary level provides services targeted on families in early difficulties such as relationship counselling for couples, informal family centres, and home visiting schemes by voluntary agencies to help families with young children. At the third or tertiary level, work with families can include those who are suffering severe difficulties and on the threshold of care proceedings characterised by intensive work either by the statutory or voluntary sector to prevent family breakdown. These three levels can be roughly compared with the four-tier CAMHS structure described in Chapter 1 and parallel the tariff of seriousness involved.

Some of the literature on family support describes ways of helping families that have the following common characteristics, which can all be found in common social work interventions (Sutton, 1999; Hill, 1999; Pinkerton et al., 2000):

- using listening skills
- getting alongside families
- emphasising collaboration
- developing cultural awareness
- gathering information
- recognising positives in the situation

In the government Quality Protects child and family consultation paper (DoH, 1999) the focus of attention emphasised better support and education for current and future parents as a preventive strategy. Key themes include the intention to improve advice and information to parents, achieving a reduction in child poverty, while offering financial help for working parents. The policy argues that by strengthening adult relationships and targeting serious family problems, an impact could be made on children's learning, youth offending, teenage pregnancy, and domestic violence. Improvements in these areas can all have a beneficial effect on child and adolescent mental health problems.

The Sure Start initiative aimed at children under three and their families living in disadvantaged areas is evidence of the practical implementation of the implicit preventive aspects of the policy which was based on evidence of success from the USA Head Start scheme (cited in Gross et al., 1995). This demonstrated long-term reductions in anti-social activity, marital problems, child abuse, adult mental health difficulties, and unemployment in later life, in a group of children who received the intervention, with a comparison of children who did not receive the programme.

Quantifying the impact of preventive family support work is complex and to achieve systematic results is expensive, therefore there is little in the way of evidence of long-term effectiveness. There can be few who would doubt though that supporting families and reducing internal and external stressors is more likely to decrease the prospects of child and adolescent mental health problems developing. However, there are signs that while outcome measures from the Department of Health refocusing initiative projects, for example were intangible, nevertheless small-scale projects could evidence positive changes. These were in relationships between parents and professionals, how to work in partnership and how to engage positively with parents, which all contributed to supporting families better (Robbins, 1998).

The lessons for social work practice are for emphasising empowering strategies, searching hard for creative solutions beyond narrow service-led resources, and refining relationship-building skills. This challenges the service management orthodoxy for short-term focussed assessments aimed at identifying need according to a limited range of resources provided by other agencies. It offers the opportunity to provide social workers with more satisfying work over longer time periods and gives service users the chance to feel contained and supported in a consistent and reliable way.

Parent education and training

The expansion of parent education or training programmes in the face of exponential demand for help from parents to deal with a range of difficulties from toddler tantrums to drug and alcohol addiction, has meant that this form of intervention is popular. Parent education is nowadays expected to be offered by service providers as part of a repertoire of family support measures. Studies of parent education programmes which while they are limited in number, show they can be an effective way of supporting families by improving behaviour in pre-adolescent children (Lloyd, 1999; Bourne, 1993; Miller and Prinz, 1990). They highlight the impact group-based behaviourally oriented programmes have in producing the biggest subsequent changes in children's behaviour and are perceived by parents as non-stigmatising. Programmes where both parents are involved and which include individual work with children are more likely to effect long-term changes.

However parent education programmes whilst enjoying a growth in popularity in Britain and other post-industrial countries, are generally not subject to rigorous evaluation (Pugh and Smith, 1996). Research shows that in a number of studies 50 per cent of parents continued to experience difficulties, and it is not clear to what extent changes were due to the format, the method of intervention, the group support or the practitioner's skills. High attrition rates from some programmes are attributed to practitioner variables such as their level of experience, and qualities such as warmth, enthusiasm, or flexibility (Barlow, 1998).

It may also be the case that some programmes are inappropriate for parents lacking motivation or feeling compelled to attend under the pressure of child protection concerns. Few British studies have used randomised controlled trials, that permit identification of the most beneficial elements of a programme, and because most provision is geared to rectifying problems in disadvantaged groups the available research evidence reflects that bias. Those that have been conducted are yielding important qualitative data from stakeholder's perspectives illustrating what is acceptable and helpful (Morrow, 1998; Ghate and Daniels, 1997). These studies are important to improving the quality of the evidence base on which to make intervention decisions.

For example, a recent study found that parenting styles have an influence on whether young teenagers age 12–13 years engage in delinquent or anti-social activity (Smith et al., 2001). The study linked smoking and drinking to delinquency, and identified a substantial use of drugs in the age group. It also suggested that young people who had been victims of bullying, robbery or assault were more likely to commit offences. Researchers measured three personality dimensions: impulsivity, alienation, and self-esteem. Those who were victimised and those who offended tended to have lower self-esteem. The study concluded that young people who witness parenting as arbitrary and inconsistent have a higher incidence of delinquency. This compares with parents who supervise children closely, but are happy to negotiate some degree of autonomy, are more likely to avoid teenage difficulties. Evidence such as this can help social workers fine-tune interventions to particular groups of young people.

Parenting education or training programmes seem to be a response to a demand for a variety of support, including information, child development knowledge, and skills development in managing children of all ages. It is a role undertaken in social work practice in the context of other work most likely general family assessments or specific risk assessments where concerns have reached the threshold of statutory intervention. The gap between the demand and provision is currently met in the voluntary and private sector that are absorbing more and more complex work with fewer qualified staff. Yet social work skills deployed early enough are ideally suited to provide appropriate family support grounded in psycho-social theory and based on best practice evidence.

Families for whom parent education is unlikely to be a sufficient response to child management difficulties are those which feature maternal depression, socio-economic disadvantage and the social isolation of the mother. Extra-familial conflict combined with relationship problems, also contribute to the problem severity and chronicity, and therefore affect the ability to introduce change. Parental misperception of the deviance of their children's behaviour is also a significant impediment to engaging in constructive family support (Macdonald and Roberts, 1995). In other words simply referring any parent/carer to a parent education resource, or offering to convene a group to parents/carers who cannot make use of the experience, is offering false hope. It can emphasise feelings of hopelessness and failure, reinforce guilt, and undermine the relationship between client and social worker.

Early intervention

The evidence demonstrates conclusively that one of the biggest risk factors in developing adult mental health problems is a history of untreated or inadequately supported childhood mental health problems (DoH, 1998; Howe, 1999; DoH, 2001). Therefore it is imperative that social work addresses this growing problem and offers its own distinctive contribution in the context of early intervention practice, the government's health improvement programme, and social services modernisation agenda. Early intervention is often synonymous with preventive practice and no more so than in child and adolescent mental health work (Walker, 2001). An even earlier preventive focus yet to be researched fully is in premarital counselling which offers the chance for couples to enhance problem-solving and decision-making skills that have the potential for learning strategies to mitigate difficulties (Stahmann, 2000).

The principle of preparing people for potential difficulties is useful and resonates with pro-active initiatives in schools, youth clubs and resources such as telephone helplines/internet discussion groups and campaigns, to reach out to children and young people *before* they reach a crisis. Linking specific social work interventions with agreed outcomes is problematic due to the network of variables potentially impacting on a child or young person's development. It is notoriously hard to accurately predict the effect of specific interventions especially when there is a lack of a research and evaluation culture in an agency. Equally it is even harder to measure the impact of preventive or early intervention programmes because of the impossibility of proving that something did not happen.

Children and adolescents acquire different at risk labels such as looked after, excluded, or young offender, affecting the variety of perceptions of their needs from the care system, education system, or youth justice system as noted in Chapter 1. This can have a detrimental effect on efforts to build a coalition among different professional staff to intervene preventively. Each professional system has its own language and methodology with which to describe the same child, sometimes resulting in friction between agencies and misconceptions about how to work together and integrate interventions. Arguments over the *real* nature of a child's behaviour or the *correct* theoretical interpretation are a wasteful extravagance. In this climate the mental health needs of such children can be neglected and the opportunity for thoughtful, preventive work missed.

As well as understanding why some children develop mental health problems, it is crucially important to learn more about those who in similar circumstances do not. Research is required to analyse the nature of these resilient children to understand whether coping strategies or skills can be transferred to other children. Positive factors such as reduced social isolation, good schooling, and supportive adults outside the family appear to help. These are the very factors missing in socially excluded families who generally live in deprived conditions and suffer more socio-economic disadvantages than other children. Yet many of these children will not develop mental health problems.

One of the most important preventive approaches is helping children and young people cope with the stresses they face in modern society. Every generation has to negotiate the manifestations of stress in their wider culture therefore relying on ways used by former generations is not useful. This is challenging to social workers who will naturally draw from their own experiences as an instinctive resource. However, the evidence suggests first in understanding the different levels of stress experienced by children and young people. Stress is a broad concept and includes a diverse range of experiences. The key is to ensure that the child themselves can categorise the level of stress. For example whether bereavement is an acute or moderate stress, or whether parental separation/divorce is a severe and longer-lasting stress. What helps is enabling the child or adolescent to focus on what can be done to improve the situation rather than concentrating on negative feelings (Rutter, 1995).

The Department of Health refocusing children's services initiative, together with the Quality Protects programme, and new Assessment guidance, are all evidence of a policy shift prompted by research into family support services and the limitations of the child protection system designed to influence social work education, training, practice, and improve effectiveness (DoH, 1995, 1999, 2000; Thoburn et al., 1998; Statham, 2000). The benefits for preventive, psycho-social work in the area of child and adolescent mental health are likely to be positive. Reducing the likelihood of mental health problems reduces the likelihood of abuse from parent/carers inability to cope.

The argument that a psycho-social perspective using psycho-dynamic skills is in diametrical contrast with an empowering approach to social work practice is unhelpful. Any model of practice has within it the potential to disempower or liberate depending on *how* it is employed by the individual social worker. There is nothing intrinsically dis-empowering about psycho-dynamic skills, or empowering about advocacy skills if they are misused or fail to connect in a meaningful way with the needs of the service user. A more sophisticated discourse is beginning to be articulated, in a way that challenges the compartmentalising of social work knowledge, theory and values, in order to stretch the boundaries of practice possibilities (Parton, 1994; Payne, 1997; Leonard, 1997; Lane, 1997; Pease and Fook, 1999). It is not inconsistent to embrace the notion that social work practice in child and adolescent mental health can shift to a more community-oriented, service-user influenced, psycho-social model that is empowering.

This proposed synthesis is not especially new. The Seebohm Report (HMSO,

1968) put forward a radical view of the role of personal social services that envisaged organisational and philosophical changes to the preceding fragmented, inadequate provision:

> *We recommend a new local authority department providing a community based and family oriented service which will be available to all. This new department will, we believe reach far beyond the discovery and rescue of social casualties: it will enable the greatest possible number of individuals to act reciprocally giving and receiving service for the well being of the whole community.* (p1).

Combining a psycho-social model with community practice is not the contradiction it might superficially appear. As the organisational framework of health and social welfare is being modernised, the opportunity arises for intellectual agility on the part of social workers. Multi-disciplinary, cross-boundary, interprofessional working is the current *credo* and it provides social workers with the potential to influence its effectiveness. Children and adolescents with mental health problems require creative and flexible solutions to their pain and suffering (Davis et al., 1997; McGuire et al., 1997; Bayley, 1998; Davis and Spurr, 1998). The onus is on social workers to draw from the deep reservoir of their knowledge and skills, and apply them in contemporary circumstances, to meet the needs of these troubled children in an accessible and socially inclusive way.

Empowering intervention

Services geared towards the needs of specific age groups of children or young people, or adults can determine the type of help offered and whether it is perceived as family or individual support (Walker, 2001a). While age is one factor, the type of problem, its degree and duration will also determine where and how help might be offered. Social workers practising in an empowering or participatory way will strive to find, or offer themselves as the most acceptable and accessible type of intervention resource. However, dilemmas will present themselves when some parents and/or children and young people express rigid views about what they want against the best available evidence of what can help.

For example a parent might insist on a child receiving individual counselling to quell troublesome behaviour, whereas all the evidence points towards couple/marital counselling. In specialist settings social workers are sometimes rejected because parents insist on a consultation with a psychiatrist-even though this may reinforce their beliefs that their child is the one with the problem. This may inhibit engaging with them in a partnership approach designed to widen their field of vision from scapegoating a child who may be simply displaying the symptoms of familial/marital or environmental causes. These beliefs and perceptions are rooted in a number of factors such as professional status/wanting the best for their child, but they are also driven by deep feelings of guilt, anxiety, fear, and anger. Using a psycho-social model social workers can respectfully address these in classic congruent, empathic, unconditional positive regard (Rogers, 1951).

Drawing on the traditions of social work practice in specialist child and adolescent mental health settings, it is possible to describe a model of contemporary intervention that can complement the organisational changes currently being implemented throughout CAMHS nationally. Such a model is based on psycho-social principles, but applied in the context of a community-oriented perspective. It is a model that can be utilised by social workers in a variety of contexts – not necessarily specialist or non-statutory. Social workers constrained by the limitations of the care management role, or repetitive assessment work, could find such a model both satisfying professionally, and more effective. Used creatively and flexibly such a model can embrace client/service user perceptions and respectfully challenge them with a menu of acceptable methods that can engage them cognitively, psychically, and practically.

Without such a holistic tool there is a risk of colluding with neglectful parents and failing to identify emerging mental health problems. The association of child mental health with a medical/pathological labelling process, or genuinely believing that only the parents require support to cope with their child's moods and behaviour, could disadvantage children. A psycho-social model of social work practice offers the optimum framework to take account of the entire individual child, family, and environmental variables interacting to produce the identified difficulties. The model offers practitioners the opportunity to apply a flexible framework within which they can choose the appropriate method of assessment and intervention themselves, or contribute to multi-disciplinary collaborative work, and evaluate the work of other professional or volunteer staff in the community (DoH,1989, 2000).

The original characteristics of a psycho-social model of social work are typically described as understanding the person as well as the problem they are presenting. This means adopting a framework that accepts the notion of the inner and outer worlds of the service user which may be in conflict and result in repetitive, self-destructive behaviour (Woods and Hollis, 1990). While this framework has a strong identification with psycho-dynamic methods of application, it is unhelpful to characterise it as narrow Freudianism or imply it is antipathetic to the needs of black and working class clients.

What it does is offer another resource to consider with clients, whether adults or children, whose anxiety, defence mechanisms, and personal difficulties are hampering their attainment of fulfilling relationships with others and hindering effective development. Recognition of the feelings underlying these behaviours offers a rich source of material to work with. Social work practice based on a psycho-social model therefore (Stepney and Ford, 2000):

- Concentrates on the present rather than the past.
- Attempts to help people achieve equilibrium between their inner emotional states and the pressures they face in the outside world.
- Uses the service user's relationship with the social worker actively.

However, a modern psycho-social model requires refinement to take account of the need for emphasis on culturally competent, empowering, and community-oriented practice. Eurocentric assumptions about normative standards of behaviour against which to assess psychological functioning have been criticised as dismissive of black and other ethnic minority constructions of self-identity and development (Robinson, 1995). These criticisms can be applied to any social work model of practice that relies on stereotyped, one-dimensional assessment. The advantage of such a refined model is both the explicit inclusively, and the importance of an examination of feelings generated during the helping process.

Reflective practice is considered to be the hallmark of modern social work practice and indeed that of other professionals working with people in a helping role. It has resonance with the ideas contained in psycho-dynamic skills of practitioner self-awareness and the feelings generated in the helping relationship between social worker and service user. It is recommended as a way of evaluating the impact of intervention and done in partnership can be empowering for some clients. Reflective critical practice is considered a preferred *modus* of work if reflective practice on its own does not question the world as it is (Adams et al., 2002). However, good reflective practice by its very nature is transformational in its questioning and evaluative stance.

Supervision or professional consultation in the area of child and adolescent mental health is a crucial component of reflective practice. A manager with the skills to offer case consultation combined with management supervision is ideal but probably a rarity. Social workers involved with families or in situations where child mental health problems are an issue require quality consultation separate from the administrative and managerial aspects of their work. A senior colleague or other professional might be the best resource as long as they can help the social worker disentangle their own feelings from those being generated during intense work. Simple concepts such as transference and projection used in a pragmatic way can go a long way towards increasing effectiveness and clarity in confusing and worrying situations.

A child's behaviour could be assessed as genetic predisposition by a physician, a specific disease requiring treatment by a psychiatrist, cognitive distortions by a psychologist, repressed unconscious desires by a child psychotherapist, or a consequence of environmental disadvantage by a social worker. It is therefore important for social workers to acquire knowledge and understanding of these potentially competing narrative understandings and theoretical paradigms (Lask and Lask, 1981; Coulshed and Orme, 1998; Hacking, 1999; Taylor and White,

2000). The challenge is to reflect on them in a sceptical, uncertain and inquisitive stance, in order to open new possibilities with colleagues and generate a range of resources to apply to the situation they are seeking to help (Parton and O'Byrne, 2001). Taking a community-oriented, psycho-social perspective enables social workers, uniquely, to place a child and young person's behaviour in a context, which can synthesise and evaluate all the potential explanations, offered by other professionals.

Case illustration

Consider the following case scenario and decide which model/s of intervention might be most useful to the family:

Paul, a five-year-old has been accommodated for two months at the request of Lucy his mother, following bruising to his right leg and right upper arm. She lost her temper after Paul had a tantrum and allegedly held and shook him strongly. Kayleigh is two and a half years old and lives with her mother. Previously perceived as a happy child developing normally, her behaviour now seems to be regressing. Byron is an eight-year-old with a history of aggressive behaviour towards other children at school. He recently started stealing money from Lucy and lighting matches around the flat.

Lucy is 25-years-old and is currently in a relationship with Kayleigh's father. Paul and Byron have different fathers who are not involved with them. Lucy is expecting her fourth child in five months time. She finds it hard to cope and is asking for help. She has poor health and a past history of physical and sexual abuse. Lucy was in care herself from five to eight years of age and is isolated from family and friends. A multi-agency review meeting has recommended immediate action. *Your task is to consider the elements of assessment and intervention required to address the mental health needs and child protection issues in this situation.*

Commentary

The primary aim of this intervention is to assist the decision-making process about Paul's future, and gain an understanding of the mental health needs of all the children. Assessing Lucy's parenting and her own need for support are priorities. This should be made explicit with Lucy and the elements of the assessment clarified so that Lucy knows what is going to happen, when, where and how.

The legal context needs to be explained and the possibility of Paul returning home or care proceedings being commenced. The assessment could be used in evidence but any hint of threat or coercion should be avoided.

An empowering approach would explain the rights of Lucy to decline to participate in the assessment, even though this might precipitate care proceedings. The areas for assessment need to be discussed and negotiated so that Lucy's concerns can be acknowledged and valued and what she is expected to achieve is made explicit.

The assessment should include what impact the child protection system has had on the family and acknowledge that their functioning will be affected in that context. A wider focus will include the current role of the grandparents and children's fathers and what support they might be prepared to offer in future.

The details of the plan for assessment and intervention can be incorporated into a written agreement. Lucy should be encouraged to obtain legal or other expert advice throughout the process to ensure she is fully aware of her rights and responsibilities. She should be able to contribute formally to the final report and express any disagreements or alternative interpretations.

A combination of various models for different aspects of the intervention process might be appropriate, as would using other professionals in contact with the family, to contribute their perspective and skills. For example, a psychodynamic model could help explore with Lucy the effects of past experiences on her current parenting capacity. A task-centred model could assist in mapping out the steps necessary for Paul's return. Individual counselling/play therapy with the other children could help enable them to manage their feelings, while a systems model could enable all the important aspects of the family's context to be included.

Methods and models of practice

The following methods and models of practice are not unique to social work nor are they an exclusive list. They have been chosen from the range of modern methods and models available to aid clarity in selection of the most appropriate components of an effective social work intervention in child and adolescent mental health work (Doel and Marsh, 1992; Payne, 1997; Coulshed and Orme, 1998; Milner and O'Byrne, 1998). Discussion of the merits of defining methods and models of social work and examination of the distinctions between terms such as practice approach, orientation and perspective, has been avoided for the sake of brevity and in order to avoid adding to the confusion already highlighted in the literature (Trevithick, 2000).

Systemic practice

Employing a systemic or systems model in child and adolescent mental health practice will be characterised by the key notion that individual children and young people have a social context which will be influencing to a greater or lesser extent, their behaviour and their perception of their problem. An important social context is that of the family and this has led to the practice of family therapy as a method of practice. It offers a broad framework for intervention enabling the mapping of all of the important elements affecting families as well as a method of working with those elements to effect beneficial change. Key features include:

- Convening family meetings to give voice to everyone connected to an individuals problem (e.g. family group conferences).
- Constructing a geneogram (family tree) with a family to help identify the quality of relationships.
- Harnessing the strengths of families to support individuals in trouble.
- Using a problem-oriented style to energise the family to find their own solutions.
- Assisting in the development of insight into patterns of behaviour and communication within the family system.
- Adopting a neutral position as far as possible in order to avoid accusations of bias or collusion.

Many professionals use this model as an overarching framework to help guide their practice. It is particularly helpful in clarifying situations where there is multi-agency and multi-professional involvement in client's lives. It can help draw boundaries and sort out who does what in, often complex, fast-moving and confusing situations. It also helps avoid the assumption that the individual child or young person is necessarily the main focus for intervention.

Disadvantages

It can be difficult for some families to appreciate the interconnectedness of the problems of individual children with wider influences. It is a way of viewing the position, role and behaviour of various individuals within the context of the whole system, but in so doing can appear abstract, culturally insensitive, and disempowering. Used uncritically it can negate the importance of individual work, as well as avoiding location of responsibility in child abuse situations.

Psycho-dynamic practice

The model offers a concept of the mind, its mechanisms, and a method of understanding why some children behave in semmingly repetitive, destructive ways. It is an essential one-to-one helping relationship involving advanced listening and communication skills. It provides a framework to address profound disturbances and inner conflicts within children and adolescents around issues of loss, attachment, anxiety, and personal development. Key ideas such as defence mechanisms, and the transference in the relationship between worker and client, can be extremely helpful in reviewing the work being undertaken, and in the process of supervision. The model helps evaluate the strong feelings aroused in particular work situations, where for example a client transfers feelings and attitudes onto the worker that derive from an earlier significant relationship.

Counter-transference occurs when the social worker tries to live up to that expectation and behave for example, like the clients parent. Key features include:

- It is a useful way of attempting to understand seemingly irrational behaviour.
- The notion of defence mechanisms is a helpful way of assessing male?
- It acknowledges the influence of past events/attachments and can create a healthy suspicion about surface behaviour.
- The development of insight can be a particularly empowering experience to enable children and young people to understand themselves and take more control over their own lives.
- The model has influenced a listening, accepting approach that avoids over-directiveness.
- It can be used to assess which developmental stage is reflected in the child or young person's behaviour and to gauge the level of anxiety/depression.

Disadvantages

The conventional criticisms of this model are its genesis in a medical model of human behaviour that relies on expert opinion without too much account of the person in their socio-economic context. In its original, uncritical form it pathologises homosexuality and negates gender power relationships. It is not considered an appropriate way of working with some ethnic minority groups and on its own cannot adequately explain the effects of racism.

Behavioural practice

Practice with this model is based on the key concept that all behaviour is learned and therefore available to be unlearned or changed. It offers a framework for assessing the pattern of behaviour in children and adolescents and a method for altering their thinking, feeling, and behaviour. The intervention can be used with individuals and groups of young people. It aims to help them become aware of themselves, link thoughts and emotions, and enable them to acquire new life skills. Using this approach social workers can decide on the new behaviours to be achieved with the client, those that are clear but also capable of measurement. Key features include:

- Using the ABC formula – what are the Antecedents, the Behaviour and the Consequences of the problem.
- Focusing on what behaviours are desired and reinforcing them.
- Modelling and rehearsing desired behavioural patterns.
- Combining behavioural and cognitive approaches to produce better results.
- Gradually desensitising a child or young person to a threat or phobia.

Behavioural approaches have appeal for staff undertaking intervention because it offers a systematic, scientific approach from which to structure their practice. The approach goes some way towards encouraging participatory practice, discouraging labelling, and maintains the client's story as central. The idea of learned helplessness has the potential to bridge the gap between psychological and sociological explanations of behaviour, maintaining the focus on both social and individual factors.

Disadvantages

Usually it is only the immediate environment of the child that is examined. It is not as value-free as it claims. The scientific nature of behavioural assessment rests on *modernist* assumptions about certainty. There is often in practice a tendency to rush a solution after a limited assessment where the theory is bent so that the individual client changes to accommodate their circumstances rather than the other way round. The potential to use the theory to employ anti-oppressive practice is limited because much of the theory is based on white, male, western norms of behaviour.

Task centred practice

Task centred work is often cited as the most popular base for contemporary assessment and intervention practice, but it may be that it is used as a set of activities rather than as a theoretically-based approach from which a set of activities flows. Key features include:

- It is based on client agreement or service user acceptance of a legal justification for action.
- It aims to move from problem to goal, from what is wrong to what is needed.
- It is based around tasks which are central to the process of change and which aim to build on individual service user strengths as far as possible.
- The approach is time-limited, preserving client self-esteem and independence as far as possible.
- It is a highly structured model of practice using a building block approach so that each task can be agreed and success or not measured by moving from problem to goal.

It can serve as a basic approach for the majority of children and young people. In this approach the problem is always the problem as defined by the client. It therefore respects their values, beliefs and perceptions. This approach encourages children and young people to select the problem they want to work on and engages them in task selection and review. It lends itself to a collaborative and empowering approach by enabling social workers to carry out their share of tasks and review them alongside the clients'. Time limits and task reviews aid motivation and promote optimism.

Disadvantages

Although this approach has the capacity for empowerment, it can sometimes prohibit active measures by practitioners to ensure it does. Although ostensibly value-free and intrinsically non-oppressive, social workers should continually reflect on their practice to make this explicit. The coaching role could be open to abuse, or permit a practitioner to become overly directive. The emphasis on simple, measurable tasks may focus attention on concrete solutions that obscure the potential advocacy role of practice. The approach requires a degree of cognitive ability and motivation in the child or young person that in some cases will be lacking.

Summary of key points

Social workers choice of intervention in child and adolescent mental health work is wide. This can be an advantage in offering the opportunity to fine-tune the right approach for the right problem to the right child. The disadvantage is that under pressure of work and feeling constrained by management timescales social workers can become bogged down in choosing the intervention, leading to confusion and ineffectiveness.

Family support in all its manifestations is an underrated but potentially powerful preventive intervention in CAMHS. It is a flexible approach that can be applied in a variety of contexts by practitioners with different levels of skill depending on the level of severity of the problem. It covers individual support for children or adults, groupwork, and community work and can encourage multi-disciplinary collaboration consistent with government policy.

Parent education and training is becoming a widespread form of intervention that is demanded by parents themselves in the face of problems with children's emotions and behaviour. The evidence is that it can be effective-but not for every family, and care needs to be used when assessing those parents likely to benefit.

Early intervention to prevent problems arising or getting worse is the desirable format for a long term response to tackling the problem of child and adolescent mental health. However, prevention cannot be proven and there are issues around targeted or universal provision that have cost implications and discriminatory consequences.

A modern and refined psycho-social model of social work practice that is community-focused and enriched with participatory, culturally competent values offers a framework to accommodate the variety of approaches and preferences of social workers interested in child and adolescent mental health.

CHAPTER 6

Inter-professional and Multi-disciplinary Care

Introduction

There is growing interest in the further development of inter-professional and multi-disciplinary working in order to maximise the effectiveness of interventions to meet the diverse needs of multi-cultural societies and service users (Magrab et al., 1997; Oberheumer 1998; Tucker et al., 1999). The evidence suggests there are cost-benefit advantages if duplication of tasks can be avoided, relationships between staff are improved and there is more opportunity to maintain the child at the centre of attention rather than the needs of the various organisations. It has been estimated for example, that between the ages of 10 and 28, young people with a conduct disorder each cost over £100,000 more in services used than those without a conduct disorder (Knapp and Scott, 1998). The suggestion is that rather than passing the young person round the system of costly service provision for repeated assessments, it would be preferable to sustain work over a *consistent* period with as few staff that *need* to be involved. Research with young people supports this proposition (Sinclair et al., 1995). What young people say they want is:

- Continuity of input from the same social worker.
- Persistence from their social worker working on their behalf.
- Social workers to engage with them in direct work.
- Social workers being less dependent on input from other professionals.

The terminology employed by staff in key agencies is one of the factors militating against more effective inter-professional work as noted in Chapter 1. Health professionals tend to talk about mental health problems and psychiatric disorders. Education staff talk about children who are presenting challenging behaviour, emotional or behavioural problems, or who have special educational needs. Social workers talk about children in need, at risk, suffering significant harm or some of the above. All these terms are used to describe children with broadly similar problems. A boy can be described by a psychiatrist as having a conduct disorder, while a teacher might say he is aggressive and attention seeking, while a social worker might describe the same boy as emotionally disturbed.

The dominance of psychiatrists and their relationships with other staff in child and adolescent mental health is a factor that needs to be considered by social workers in specialist or non-specialist settings whether working closely together or occasionally in case review meetings. It is easy to be overawed by the status and power of psychiatrists who can sometimes assume they are managing a case. If legal proceedings are involved their evidence will have a particular and prominent status in court. Psychiatric intervention in the field of child and adolescent mental health includes treatment covering all therapeutic and pharmacological approaches used for children with emotional and behavioural disturbances. It is important to bear in mind that psychiatrists, whatever their particular interest in cognitive-behavioural, psycho-analytical or family therapy approaches, are *doctors* and have trained in a *medical model* of understanding human growth and development. Social workers need not seek conflict with this concept but rather ensure that their social model of understanding is placed alongside it.

Inter-professional relationships

The characteristics of successful multi-disciplinary work occur within a framework familiar to social workers. It begins with assessment then proceeds through decision-making, planning, monitoring, evaluation, and finally to closure. It is argued that this common framework employed by most health and social care staff, offers the optimum model for encouraging reflective practice to be at the core of contemporary social work (Taylor and White, 2000). This can occur in an examination of the impact of the intervention in meeting the child's needs; the evaluation of staff inputs and strategies; and the relationship between organisational demands, resources, objectives and priorities. Each agency involved can measure effectiveness against this basic framework and find common ground on which to consider the best way of helping a troubled child or adolescent.

Reflective practice in work with child and adolescent mental health problems offers the opportunity to shift beyond functional analysis to making active links between the value base, policy-making process, and the variety of interventions conducted. Combined with this practice-led motivation for inter-professional working, there is evidence that government policy imperatives requiring closer co-operation between professionals coming into contact with children and families are having an effect (Eber et al., 1996; Vandenberg and Grealish, 1996; Sutton, 2000). Social workers skills in relationship-building, their tendency to make links, network and share information, make them ideally suited to advance this agenda.

The aim is for a seamless web of provision from primary through to tertiary care where needs are recognised, assessed and interventions formulated on a preventive basis in order to stop small, manageable difficulties developing into big intractable problems. Without such early intervention within a holistic multi-factoral approach, children suffering early difficulties run the risk of becoming troubled adults with all the greater social, psychological and financial consequences that entails (Bayley, 1998). Social workers are central to the success of this project with their distinctive capacity for facilitating multi-agency co-operation.

The importance of evaluative research for child and adolescent mental health services has been emphasised by both the National Health Service Research and Development Committee (HAS, 1995) and the Audit Commission (1994). This is recommended as a way to aid multi-disciplinary work and decision-making about policy strategy and resource allocation. It is consistently emphasised that agencies need to work together to prioritise work, to establish the effectiveness of the help children and young people receive, and to identify strategies for providing effective mental health services. Only with properly constructed research designs and rigorous methodology that can analyse the factors contributing to better multi-disciplinary work, will faster progress be made on this policy aspiration.

Changing patterns of service delivery

Research conducted over the past decade by diverse independent and government sources has found child and adolescent mental health services to be fragmented, under-resourced, poorly staffed, and ill-equipped to meet the needs of increasing numbers of troubled young people with a complex variety of mental health difficulties. The following set of principles for developing synchronised models of care to respond to identified need established a framework in which specialist CAMHS are advised to operate (Wallace et al., 1995):

- The majority of problems can be dealt with in Primary Care.
- Specialists should provide support to the other groups.
- The specialist service should be convenient and appropriate for children and adolescents.
- Specialist services should include both uni-disciplinary and multi-disciplinary resources to cover the spectrum of need.
- Specialist services should be targeted on categories of children with a high prevalence of mental health problems and should be distributed to provide maximum resources at points of need.
- There should be a co-ordinating structure, with shared strategies and policies, in order to reduce duplications, gaps and confusion for users.
- No uni-disciplinary service should work in isolation. Open channels of communication and procedures providing for ready access to other levels of the service should be agreed.
- Professional isolation should be avoided and professional accountability should be to individuals within the same discipline. This should not be confused with accountability for the provision of services.
- Services should be managed so that every profession shares in the organisation of intra-professional matters, such as audit, training, supervision, recruitment, and service development.

Table 6.1: Areas for consideration when planning multidisciplinary care (after Horwath and Calder, 1998)

Initial discussion	Identify core group staff	Collate contributions to plan	Specify meeting dates	Clarify responsibility boundaries	Clarify assessment depth
The core group	Purpose and function	Methods to promote participatory practice	Anticipate potential inter-agency problems	Agree protocols for more attendees	Management of meeting-minutes feedback
The plan	Overall aim	Timescale to implement	Methods to engage child and family	Agree procedures for changes to plan	Evaluation and plan monitoring
The key worker	Co-ordination	Direct work with child or family	Keeping an overview	Clarify joint working tasks	Manage inter-agency problems
The review	The remit of the review	Delegation of core group decisions	Guidance on reporting to the review	Enabling contributions from child and family	Providing support to staff

The organisational patterns for service delivery across all public services are now moving to multi-professional, multi-disciplinary and cross-departmental teams in order to reduce or eliminate such blockage. This is in effect, what is meant by government reference to cross-cutting approaches to the delivery of public services. In health and social care, this translates into multi-agency working and there are signs of new inter-professional teams being created. Ovretveit (1996) argues that it is important to be able to distinguish the type of multidisciplinary team so that:

- Practitioners understand their role.
- Managers can make changes to improve service quality.
- Planners can decide which type is most suited to the needs of a client population.
- Researchers can contribute to knowledge about which type is most effective.

Joint practitioner teams in health and social services can be described in three broad ways. The first refers to *the degree of integration or closeness of working between professions*. One way of achieving integration is the development of a core training programme for all staff. This would cover a range of relevant subjects for example:

- child and adolescent mental health
- attachment theory
- emotional impact of divorce and separation
- child protection
- child development
- domestic violence
- resilient children
- preventive work
- bereavement and loss
- parenting skills
- anti-discriminatory practice
- Human Rights Act
- children's rights

Apart from increasing the knowledge and skills base of individual practitioners who came with different levels of prior training and staff development, the delivery mode of the training would not be profession-specific and thus unlike much conventional training. It would also be delivered not just to whole teams but to the whole CAMH service. The additional benefit of such a system-wide training programme would be closer integration within teams and across the local service. This concept is already manifesting to some extent with the example of the joint practitioner in learning disability, with original qualification in, for example, nursing and social work (Davis et al., 1999). Also, the new joint commissioning environment in health and social care enshrined in the Health Act (DoH, 1999) enables new services to be created where multi-disciplinary working is enhanced.

The second way of describing joint practitioner teams refers to *the extent to which the team manages its resources as a collective and permanent presence, or as separate professional services.* One of the vexed questions about effectiveness in the organisation of interprofessional care is how to mitigate the impact of the structural inhibitors thwarting attempts to cut across professional boundaries. These can be exemplified by the variety of geographical boundaries covered by health, social services and education authorities, combined with different pay scales and terms of employment (Young and Haynes, 1993; Leathard, 1994). In child and adolescent mental health services the Education, Health and Social Work structural hierarchies have traditionally militated against collaboration; preserved separate professional role identities; and inhibited inter-professional working (Fagin, 1992; Rawson, 1994; DfEE, 1998).

This has thwarted repeated attempts to achieve the much-vaunted seamless service for children and families in difficulties as recommended in the Children Act (DoH, 1989). This problem can be overcome at the planning stage by providing each local service with a specific geographical catchment area based on the Primary Care Trust boundaries. This enables creative innovative thinking to flourish within and between agencies.

The third way of describing joint practitioner teams refers to *how the team is led and how its members are managed.* Team management is a potentially controversial subject where the challenge in multi-disciplinary teams is to establish a structure that allows appropriate autonomy for practitioners from different professions but permits the team manager to control the use of staff time (Onyet et al., 1994). The professional background of such a manager will invariably cause concerns about favouritism or bias towards those from a similar background. Old rivalries and jealousies could quickly surface and threaten team harmony and collaborative working.

The job of manager therefore calls for highly developed diplomatic skills internally and externally, in relation to other agencies. Generally, there needs to be information cascade within the CAMHS tiered structure and outside into the broader children and families services framework. This is necessary to ensure more fluid communication between agencies in order to ensure as far as possible that the right service is supporting the right families at the right time. Within a focused CAMHS strategy, it is a crucial management task to liaise with other services providers in efforts to achieve the following:

- To streamline the referral processes between each service.
- To exchange referrals and share in consultation.
- To avoid families or referrers feeling passed around the system.
- To maintain service accountability.

- To monitor service eligibility criteria.

The multi-disciplinary nature of CAMH services offering intensive input, advice, information, parental guidance, and direct work with children in their own homes, or in preferred contexts such as schools, are indicative of a non-stigmatising acceptable service. The issue of roles and boundaries between different professionals has long been debated in the literature on health and social care and there is evidence that change is happening (Munley et al., 1982; NISW, 1982). For example the contemporary *mode* for joined up working and inter-professional care has promoted joint training and qualifications in working with people with learning disabilities and adults with mental health problems.

Recent initiatives to expand the role of nurses and social workers contribute to a blurring of roles often approved by clients (Snelgrove and Hughes, 2000; Williams et al., 1999; Pearce, 1999). The stigma of child and adolescent mental health deters many young people from gaining access to the right help at the right time. Combined with the profound feelings of guilt experienced by some parents, which prevents them seeking support, means there is enormous unmet need in the community. Initiatives to bring together different professionals in offering a more accessible, appropriate, and acceptable service for troubled young people and their families is required to respond to a growing problem. Early intervention over a short period of time, with an eclectic mix of staff offering practical, therapeutic, activity based help, and advice, is one viable part of an overall strategy.

Overcoming the hurdles to implementation

Despite understanding the challenges to multi-disciplinary working and having a better organisational framework there are still hurdles to overcome in order to implement working together principles. While there is evidence of the positive benefits of skill mix and sharing knowledge thus leading to a blurring of former professional identities, there is other evidence that paradoxically, the encouragement of generic inter-professional working actually *reinforces* boundaries between professions (Brown et al., 2000). It is possible that as staff continue to train together, develop generic working and eventually harmonise status and pay differentials, there may be some resistance to relinquishing former roles, and there may even be a *strengthening* of the boundaries between professions. The challenge for the managers will be to preserve the distinctive individual professional expertise base, but not at the expense of service coherence. The challenge for practitioners will be to maintain a sense of loyalty to an identity while at the same time enabling that identity to change. Table 6.1 provides an illustration of the areas for consideration when planning multi-disciplinary care for a child.

Services targeted at areas of social disadvantage where high levels of truancy, school exclusion, child protection registrations, juvenile crime, unemployment, and emerging child mental health problems can be identified, and support the social exclusion agenda of the government. But it is necessary to ensure the representative nature of the workforce in terms of gender, ethnic diversity, and disability. The literature on race and gender emphasises the importance of balance and proportionality with regard to the demographic nature of the area being served. Yet all the evidence suggests that in children and families' welfare services there are unrepresentative and disproportionate numbers of female white middle class professional staff (Dominelli, 1996; Cote, 1997; Bhugra, 1999; Bhugra and Bahl, 1999).

The profile of social and health care teams working in child and adolescent mental health services largely reflects the professional white female population. There is some evidence that more male staff may help some boys and young men to engage more effectively with service provision. Clearly there is a dilemma in trying to achieve balanced inter-professional team membership with the need to maintain appropriate levels of expertise. This is not a problem unique to child and adolescent mental health services, but there is ample evidence that these factors weigh heavily when attempting to engage children and families already suffering under the pressure of racism and/or discrimination (Bhui and Olajide, 1999). It is important that children, families and carers have maximum choice when engaging with services aiming to meet their needs, and as discussed in Chapter 4, *as important* not to assume that black families only require black staff.

In addition, child and adolescent mental health services would benefit from formal service user involvement, especially children and young people separately from parents or carers, at the clinical audit, monitoring, review, and strategic planning levels of the service (Alderson, 2000; Barnes and Warren, 1999; Treseder, 1997). There is less of a tradition of such involvement in medical practice than in social work practice. Dissolving the boundaries between professionals carries with it the implication for narrowing the gap between service user and practitioner. Some of the contemporary literature on child and adolescent mental health service development is debating the ethical, professional and practical issues raised in considering how to genuinely engage service users-*especially children themselves*, as partners in the process (Walker, 1999; Kent and Read, 1998; Nixon and Northrup, 1997; Walker, 2001).

The practical results of efforts to encourage inter-professional working aiming to improve the quality, delivery and co-ordination of all services for children and young people, need to be rigorously evaluated (DoH, 1998; Tucker et al., 1999; Rodney, 2000). In the history of child and adolescent mental health services there has always been a recognition that multi-disciplinary effort needs to be brought to bear on the difficulties of troubled children. That model has now been updated with initiatives such as, for example, Family Support Teams functioning to fulfil an inter-professional role within a CAMHS struggling to cope with increased demand (Walker, 2000).

This model could be the genesis for a new primary mental health care professional, within a preventive configuration, with implications for training, qualifications, accreditation, and employment which demonstrably reflects an inter-professional perspective. They would be the embodiment of inter-professional working and an attractive prospect for social workers keen to use helping skills in direct work. The concept of early intervention is critical in child and adolescent mental health because there are few opportunities to make an impact in the developmental windows of opportunity that present in young people, before problems become entrenched. Primary mental health care staff intervening successfully at the appropriate moment could reduce vulnerability to later mental health problems in adulthood, with all the social, inter-personal, and economic savings for those individuals, their families, and society.

Primary mental health care practitioners are already beginning to be appointed within CAMHS and could eventually be the professional glue to hold the four-tier structure together. Working to bridge the gap between primary care and specialist care in child and adolescent mental health services they come from a multi-disciplinary range of professional backgrounds and are positioning themselves to strengthen and support CAMHS provision by a variety of means:

- Early recognition and intervention in CAMH problems.
- Helping other staff make informed decisions about potential referrals.
- Joint working in assessment of needs.
- Supporting teachers with consultancy and advice.
- Offering education and training to primary care staff.
- Working directly with children and young people or parents/carers.
- Consolidating primary care staff skills in identification and management of CAMH issues.
- Providing an effective gateway to specialist support or SEN assessment.

Case illustration

A referral has been made to your child and family team by a teacher at a primary school concerning Jake, an eight-year-old boy. His behaviour is described as out of control, refusal to comply with instructions and aggression towards other pupils. He comes from a well-off family who live in owner-occupied property where both parents work full-time. An older sibling, Francesca, took a non-fatal overdose of paracetamol 11 months ago when she was 14 years old and was seen briefly by the nearest child and family consultation service.

The CFCS report by the consultant psychiatrist said Francesca had been seriously depressed for some time before the overdose. She has been prescribed anti-depressant medication. The psychiatrist described the parents as rigid disciplinarians with low warmth towards their children. Mother is believed to be an alcoholic and father works 14-hour days regularly in his own business. *You have been asked to make a provisional plan of action involving inter-professional and multi-disciplinary working.*

Commentary

Inter-professional and multi-disciplinary working will be crucial to the success of this case. Already there are potentially three or four different agencies with the possibility of six different professionals involved – teacher and educational psychologist in school; psychiatrist and therapist from CFCS; and social workers from children and family team and adult community mental health team.

   Clarifying case management and staff lines of accountability early on could save embarrassment or more serious problems later on. Make sure who does what and when with whom is recorded in accordance with an agreed plan. The social worker in the children and family team is likely to be expected to be the key worker and co-ordinator.

   Agreeing a provisional plan and noting the variety of hypotheses, interpretations or explanations for the behaviour of the children needs to be done skilfully with balance and respect for the diversity of opinion likely to be expressed. For example a provisional diagnosis of ADHD in Jake needs to be thoroughly assessed because of the impact such a label might have on all the stakeholders involved. The hard part is to match these ideas with what is required in terms of support or therapy, and whether the resources are there to provide it. Issues of gender and culture need to be openly addressed in terms of the family process and the tasks for different professionals.

   The parents are crucial allies in this work. They must be engaged and encouraged to actively participate in planning and any work such as individual work with the children, family therapy, parent education, or marital counselling. They may have fixed ideas about what is needed and shy away from marital counselling, so that may need to be kept as part of a later intervention as the case's natural history unfolds. They have seen medication work with Francesca and may press for a popular amphetamine-based medication to be prescribed for Jake.

   Quick results may be achieved particularly if there is a lot of activity from a variety of professionals. The temptation will be to close the case and move on to other urgent work, however this may disguise the fact that underlying problems may have simply been covered up in the light of attention paid to the children and the reduction in the level of anxiety. Keeping professionals and families engaged at these points is difficult, but an argument for prevention of further difficulties could succeed. Sometimes though, it is useful to have laid the foundation for families to alter their perception of themselves. This could avert a future crisis by enabling them to recognise the warning signs and seek help earlier.

The place of social work

The evidence therefore supports the notion that it is possible to establish, with careful planning, inter-professional teams who are able to integrate with and mobilise primary care staff, within the social environments of children and families (Falloon and Fadden, 1995). As the evidence base for effectiveness builds in this area of work, further research will be required to examine the long-term consequences of initiatives in child and adolescent mental health service development. This can contribute to the refinement of studies into inter-professional working not just to improve CAMHS but in all other children's services.

Any model of social work practice in this area has to be able to find its place within the existing and constantly changing mosaic of professional and voluntary provision located in communities and informal networks. The challenge is to create a system of multi-disciplinary expertise and resources that are accessible and acceptable to service users, and that can work together. Internationally, there have been attempts to identify common inter-professional training needs to enable staff to work better in integrated service delivery systems (Magrab et al., 1997; DfEE, 1998).

They demonstrate that inter-professional training can reflect the aspiration that people who *work* together should also *train* together to enable a consistency of approach to the identified difficulty. It is possible to identify and design the inter-professional training needs of staff to enable them to function in integrated service delivery systems for children and young people. The conclusions are that previous policy frameworks focused on children's service planning missed the opportunity to recognise multi-disciplinary training as a priority and to provide incentives to Universities and other training institutions to develop inter-professional training programmes (DoH/DfEE,1996).

There is evidence of attempts to foster inter-professional training among primary care staff in child mental health, and overcome the institutional barriers militating against good community practice (Firth et al., 1999; Sebuliba and Vostanis, 2001). The ranges of professions potentially undertaking work with children and adolescents who have mental health problems bring different skills, training, experience and knowledge to the task. According to the NHS Advisory Service (1995) guidance suggests that irrespective of which tier of service is involved, there are some basic attributes which all members of a multi-disciplinary service or team, should possess. These are consistent with a psycho-social model of social work practice, but they may not be reflected in other professional training and education:

- Empathetic interviewing and counselling skills.
- A working knowledge of child development.
- Up to date working knowledge of child and family problems.
- Understanding of the impact of major life events on children's lives.

- Awareness of how the professional's own life experiences inform their approach to others.
- Familiarity with manifestations of serious psychiatric disorders.

The place of social work practice in child and adolescent mental health is also determined to some extent by how other professionals perceive it. Some staff will assume that the social work involvement is to take responsibility for the assessment of and legal responsibility for, child protection investigations. This is an area of potential confusion and conflict. Social workers employed in specialist CAMH services have contractual arrangements and role descriptions that do not help clarify their status with regard to child protection concerns. Equally, it is not uncommon for some other professionals to seek to avoid their duties under Area Child Protection Committee guidelines, claiming client confidentiality.

For example, a social worker involved in a therapeutic piece of work with a young person may feel the need to continue that work unhindered by responsibilities for leading a child protection investigation. In such cases they need to inform the relevant social work child protection team manager and negotiate a division of work with another social work colleague so that the needs of the child or young person for sustained support are recognised, whilst a thorough and sensitive investigation proceeds without delay. Confidentiality during therapeutic work can only be assured except where the worker becomes aware of child protection issues. Therefore how and when this confidentiality agreement is breached needs very careful handling. The cost to the child or young person's trust in the worker, the impact on further therapeutic needs, and the potential damage to their sense of integrity could be high. This has to be weighed against the quality of the evidence of abuse, the impact of the investigative and legal process, and the prospects for future protection. Only the most skilled and thoughtful supervision combined with intelligent multi-agency communication will help guide the way forward.

In less fraught situations, other professionals may assume that the role of the social worker in CAMH services is to take responsibility for welfare rights/social security matters or to negotiate with housing authorities. In some cases this might be completely appropriate and reflects how the job is specified. However, a social worker might also have advanced therapeutic qualifications in family therapy or counselling and in practice is working as a highly skilled therapist. In some situations practical issues can impede the need for intense transformational experiences that will in the long term equip children and parents with the capacity to manage those practical issues more effectively. Again, a pragmatic division of labour with a colleague can avoid unnecessary difficulties. The guiding principle as ever, is what is in the best interests of the child or young person.

Other professionals do not experience the same level of supervision or the same type of supervision that permits reflective practice. The tradition in social work of such supervision is constantly under pressure by managerialist prescriptions for brief, task-centred working practices, risk assessment and prioritisation of caseloads. However, supervision that enables a worker to understand and learn from the interactive processes experienced during work is a valuable tool to encourage social workers to reflect on child and adolescent mental health practice that can be emotionally draining. Some social workers may find the experience unsettling while others will draw immense comfort from it. Both will benefit and have their practice enhanced as a result. In multi-disciplinary and inter-professional contexts a culture of such enlightened supervision for all staff can create a rich climate for professional growth and improved quality of service to young people. The evidence suggests there is an appetite to incorporate this social work model of supervision into new multi-disciplinary CAMHS teams (Debell and Walker, 2002).

Social workers bring a distinctive contribution to inter-professional and multi-disciplinary work in child and adolescent mental health. Effective multi-disciplinary team-working or inter-agency working requires the notion of power to be addressed and shared more equally between staff. It also requires power to be shared by more participative practices with service users and the community being served. Social workers skills in advocacy and empowerment are therefore crucial in making this happen. Social workers also bring a concept of oppression and how discriminatory social contexts can blight the lives of children and families. This wider social and political perspective can raise awareness among other staff and inform and enrich the intervention practice of other professionals.

Summary of key points

Inter-professional and multi-disciplinary work is easier to avoid than engage in because of the potential for frustration, confusion, and disagreement with staff reflecting a variety of theoretical and structural positions. There is also the potential that it can offer children and adolescents an all-inclusive repertoire of help and support to contain some of the destructive emotions experienced by parents and other family members. The benefits of working together cannot be overstated but this should not happen at the expense of proper professional debate that sometimes can be difficult.

Health and social care service delivery is now built around the concept of joined up working, however translating that into meaningful practice skills and processes is hard. The pressure to spread staff thinly across a range of need may not, in the long run, prevent the mental health of some children and young people deteriorating, and only scratch the surface of other more serious problems. The social work task is to research the local community to identify naturally occurring resources/networks of people, who with support and encouragement can bring their expertise to the search for solutions.

The characteristics of successful multi-disciplinary work occur within a framework familiar to social workers. It begins with assessment then proceeds through decision-making, planning, monitoring, evaluation, and finally to closure. This common framework employed by most health and social care staff offers the optimum model for encouraging reflective practice. Each agency can measure effectiveness against this basic framework and find common ground on which to consider the best way of helping a troubled child or adolescent.

Initiatives to expand the role of other professionals and social workers contribute to a blurring of roles often approved of by clients. The stigma of child and adolescent mental health deters many young people from gaining access to the right help at the right time. Bringing together different professionals in offering early intervention in a more accessible, appropriate, and acceptable service for troubled young people and their families is required.

The practical results of efforts to encourage inter-professional working aiming to improve the quality, delivery and co-ordination of all CAMH services for troubled children and young people, need to be rigorously evaluated. Lessons learned can help improve inter-professional and multi-disciplinary working and where appropriate, be transferred to all children's services.

Social workers bring a distinctive and crucial contribution to inter-professional and multi-disciplinary care in child and adolescent mental health work. This includes awareness of oppression and discrimination against marginalised children and families created by a context of social exclusion, advanced skills in negotiation, networking and facilitating closer working together between agencies, and interpersonal communication skills used in therapeutic/counselling work with children and families. They also bring advocacy/empowerment skills to broaden the perspective of other professionals and reduce the power imbalance between them and the community they serve.

CHAPTER 7

Socially Inclusive Practice

Introduction

The term social inclusion has gained rapid acceptance within the social work literature at the beginning of the 21st century. It began to appear prominently in political discourse in the UK following the election of a Labour government in 1997 which regarded social exclusion as an impediment to its vision of a more open and equal society concerned with social justice as well as economic progress. The concept of social exclusion has its origins in France in the 1970s where the idea of citizenship and social cohesion highlighted the plight of *Les exclus* who were relegated to the margins of society (Barry and Hallett, 1998; Pierson, 2002). The social policy aim therefore is to advance a socially inclusive social and health care policy enabling any and every citizen to enjoy the opportunities offered by late capitalist Britain and the European Economic Community in an increasingly economically globalised world.

Each individual regardless of class, race, culture, age, religion, disability or gender is to find the traditional barriers to their advancement being dismantled so that nobody should be excluded from sharing in the wealth and resources being offered at a time of sustained economic expansion. These political aspirations fit with the value base of social work which embodies anti-discriminatory practice, respect for persons, and equal opportunities for every citizen. However, just as the earlier stages of capitalism resulted in new approaches to the social management of the disruption, impoverishment, and alienation of the social casualties of economic progress, so too are the late stages of capitalism (Leonard, 1997). Social workers are among those in the front line faced with the consequences of the failure of this latest social policy aspiration and the raised expectations of people in need. Part of the consequences, are the disproportionate effects on the mental health of socially excluded children and young people.

The evidence suggests that the gap between rich and poor is widening, there are more children living in poverty, the prison population is at its highest recorded level, and disabled people are more likely to live in poverty or be unemployed than non-disabled people. Children from working class families are less likely to receive a further or higher education and black families are more likely to live in poor housing. There are differences within these broad examples of social exclusion that need to be taken into account when social workers are assessing strengths, resources, and gaps in social networks where they are trying to help children and young people with mental health problems. Inner city deprivation, migration patterns, and poorer health outcomes are factors also associated with class and are therefore likely to affect any family in disadvantaged social circumstances.

The effects of social inequality

Mental health problems affect three times as many children in social class V (manual and unskilled) compared with those in social class I (professional) according to the authoritative Social Trends 32 report (ONS, 2002). It is important therefore to consider the external context of child and adolescent mental health problems and acknowledge that the impact of service provision in some families is mediated by factors such as unemployment, poor housing and poverty. They all contribute to the level of resilience and capacity for resourcefulness of children and families (Eamon, 1994; Dunn, 1999; Micklewright and Stewart, 2000). The recent report on social inequalities from the Office for National Statistics states that one in ten children in the United Kingdom suffer from a poverty related mental health problem (HMSO, 2000). According to other research the UK is fourth from the bottom of a list of relative poverty among the nineteen richest nations (UNICEF, 2000).

The present government target is to reduce child poverty by a quarter by 2004, to halve it by 2010 and to abolish it by 2021. The calculations for defining poverty, relative poverty and absolute poverty are complex and subject to much statistical interpretation and debate. The current measure for calculating relative child poverty (defined as children living in households with incomes below 50 per cent of the national median) does not reveal anything about the *depth* of poverty. In other words every household below the 50 per cent threshold would be counted regardless of whether they were just below or in complete destitution. Also it fails to measure how *long* children have lived in poverty. This is important given the cumulative psychological effects of persistent social exclusion.

Concern about the most disadvantaged socially excluded people in society provides ammunition for those whose response is to resort to criticism of the 'isms' used to draw attention to discrimination: disablism, heterosexism, racism, sexism etc. and for the charge of 'political correctness' to be deployed as a means of undermining the policy aim of achieving social justice. It may indeed be considered a measure of how successful a socially inclusive practice is becoming, the louder the voices of those vested interests who want to exclude the majority of citizens from access to the nation's resources. What the various 'isms' have in common is the core value of equal opportunity that to some is an anathema. Any effective assessment in child and adolescent mental health practice needs to consider the impact of its absence and the absence of equal access to resources (Milner and O'Byrne, 1998).

The stigma and discrimination faced by adults with mental health problems illustrate the importance of work with children and adolescents who are vulnerable to developing mental health problems. Many will overcome their difficulties especially with early intervention and the external supports and internal resilience noted in previous chapters. However, those who go on to develop mental health problems into adulthood will be among the most socially excluded people in society. Apart from their reduced access to physical health care, they will face reduced employment prospects, problems with financial services, and limited access to decent housing. Their own sense of despair and shame will force them to hide their mental health problems making them among the most physically and emotionally isolated people in society (Read and Barker, 1996; Repper et al., 1997; Sayce and Measey, 1999; Newbigging, 2001). The potential positive impact of preventive social work intervention with children and adolescents at risk of mental health problems in the context of social exclusion cannot be over-emphasised.

The following section focuses on some of the most socially excluded children and their families but is not intended to indicate any priority of need or to restrict the reader's attention from the many other groups who also suffer from social exclusion.

Socially excluded children and their families

Black children

Inspection of services for black children and their families shows that despite the years of rhetoric of anti-racist and anti-oppressive social work practice, assessments and care planning are still generally inadequate (SSI, 2000). Assessments are often partial and rarely cover parental capacity, the child's needs, and environmental issues. There is little evidence that care planning takes a lifelong view – highlighting the failure to recruit black foster carers or understanding the changing characteristics of this group of children. The mental health needs of black children are virtually ignored. The SSI guidance suggests:

- Ensuring that services and staffing are monitored by ethnicity to ensure they are provided appropriately and equally.
- Involving ethnic minorities in planning and reviewing services.
- Training in anti-racist and anti-discriminatory practice.
- Investigating and monitoring complaints of racial discrimination or harassment.
- Explicit policies are in place for working with black families.

Continual reflection and evaluation of practice is required to maintain an anti-racist socially inclusive practice. Recognising racial harassment as a child protection issue and as an indicator for subsequent potential mental health problems is evidence of the translation of policy generalisation into specific practice change. Social workers who make sure they take full account of a child's religion, racial, cultural and linguistic background in the decision making process are demonstrating the link between social policy and socially inclusive practice. Ensuring that black children in residential care have access to advocates and positive role models can assist in challenging institutionally racist practice.

A socially inclusive social work practice will help develop strategies to overcome value judgements about the superiority of white British family culture and norms. Exploring the impact of white power and privileges in social work relationships with black people and drawing connections between racism and the social control elements of social work practice, is another example. Rejecting stereotypes of black and ethnic minority family structures and relationships will enable social workers to assess the rich cultural, linguistic and spiritual diversity of family life and permit the building of an assessment not based on a deficit model judged against an anglocentric norm.

There is strong evidence that the experience of racism affects the mental health prospects of black children, therefore efforts to protect black children from racism and racist abuse is a priority within a socially inclusive practice. Recent research by the NSPCC revealed (Barter, 1999):

- Racism and racial bullying are commonplace within the lives of ethnic minority children and young people
- The most common expression of racism is through racist name-calling previously considered by adults as trivial but the impact is now known to be profound.
- Racial bullying frequently involves the use of violence.
- Violence against ethnic minority groups is persistent, patterned, and long-term in the way it affects individuals and the places where they live.

Disabled children

Disabled children and those with learning difficulties are more likely to have mental health problems than other children. Disabled children and adolescents are twice as likely to have emotional and behavioural problems. There are a growing number of disabled children and young people living in the community who need high levels of support. Partly this is because more of these children are surviving infancy, and partly because there is no longer the assumption that disabled children should be cared for in hospitals or other institutions. Lone parents with disabled children, families from ethnic minorities, and families caring for the most severely disabled children have the highest levels of unmet need, and live in the poorest conditions. The mental health needs of disabled children are often masked by a narrow focus on their disability through a medical, rather than social model of disability. Behaviour causing concern can often be ascribed to the physical or intellectual disability rather than a separate psychological need.

Disabled children with a severe disability need to know how to deal with the social and psychological challenges they face – including dealing with other family members, coping with their own negative feelings, and planning for the future (Beresford et al., 1996). Families require relief and request a range of support including home-based sitting services, residential or family-based respite care, or long-term care from social services departments. Needs change over time. For instance a family with an autistic child may want a graded range of services. In the early years they want information and support with their child's development. When the child is a bit older they need respite care. But when the children reach early teens the research says about 60 per cent of families want their child to be accommodated by the local authority.

Under part 3 of the Disability Discrimination Act 1995 social services and other service providers must not discriminate against disabled children by refusing to provide any service which is provided to other children, by providing a lower standard of service or offering a service on less favourable terms. From 2004 service providers will have to take reasonable measures to remove, alter, or provide reasonable means of avoiding physical features that make it impossible or unreasonably difficult for disabled children to use the services including when they are undertaking or contributing to assessments. This means access to child and adolescent mental health services needs to be considered from the disabled child's perspective. A socially inclusive practice would link with local disabled children's networks and involve parent/carers and children in the planning and delivery of necessary changes.

The mental health needs of deaf children like other disabled children are often overlooked or simply poorly understood. The medical model of disability ensures that the disability itself is the focus of attention rather than the disabling environment and attitudes of society. Very little research has been undertaken with this particularly socially excluded group to try to understand their emotional and psychological needs and the impact on them of their disability. Deaf culture needs to be taken into account if a socially inclusive practice is to be employed by social workers. Its principle characteristics are:

- Sharing a common language (BSL) for communication purposes.
- Social interaction choices.
- Identity issues.
- Historic understanding of discrimination.

Deaf BSL users view their deafness as a cultural identity, they are proud of their language and feel they belong to a linguistic minority group. They do not want their deafness to be cured and are more concerned about improved access to services, information and democracy. The Disability Rights Commission was established to act as a watchdog for implementation of the Disability Discrimination Act 1995. The commission would be a powerful ally to social workers seeking to ensure that the mental health needs of deaf children and young people are not hindered by the lack of specific and appropriate services.

The low uptake of respite services by Asian parents with a disabled child are still perceived by some as evidence of the closed-network of familial relationships within Asian culture, rather than evidence of the inaccessibility of existing service provision. Sometimes this is a matter of proper translating services being unavailable but it can also represent a lack of effort from social workers and other social care professionals to understand the families they aspire to help. For example, some Asian families are reluctant to have daughters cared for by male carers, or they simply have little knowledge of the health and welfare system in Britain (Shah, 1992). Even when good translators are available they do not always manage to convey the subtleties of meaning related to feelings and cultural differences. Trying to distinguish the mental health needs of children and young people with a physical or learning disability is difficult enough for many professionals let alone for black families already disadvantaged.

Young offenders

According to recent figures there were 11,500 young people aged 15 to 20 in jail in England and Wales in 2000, of those 90 per cent had a diagnosable mental health disorder, and many had substance abuse problems as well as personality disorders (Lyon et al., 2000). 60 per cent had anxiety and depressive illness with 10 per cent suffering from a severe psychotic mental illness such as schizophrenia. 20 per cent of these young men and 40 per cent of young women will have attempted suicide prior to their imprisonment (Farrant, 2001). Young offenders are among the most socially excluded groups in society and the evidence suggests that imprisonment simply makes matters worse not better. Within two years of release, 75 per cent will have been reconvicted and 47 per cent will be back in jail (Social Exclusion Unit, 2002). If some of these young people become homeless or end up in insecure accommodation, they are between eight and 11 times more likely to develop mental health problems (Stephens, 2002).

Low take up of preventive mental health services among socially excluded families means that minor problems can develop into major problems. Over 90 per cent of recidivist delinquents had a conduct disorder as children. The estimated annual cost per child if conduct disorder is left untreated is £15,270. 40 per cent of 7–8 year olds with an untreated conduct disorder became recidivist delinquents as teenagers. Young offenders are three times as likely to have a mental health problem as other young people. Yet these problems are often neglected because there are no proper methods for screening and assessing mental health problems within the youth justice system (Farrington, 1995; Goodman and Scott, 1997; Royal College of Psychiatrists, 2002; Mental Health Foundation, 2002).

The evidence shows that more than 25 per cent of young men and 41 per cent of young women under 21 in prison had received treatment for mental health problems in the year before they were jailed (Lader et al., 1997). Once in the prison system, a lack of purposeful activity, long hours in cells, and a climate of brutality and bullying can reinforce negative attitudes and magnify underlying mental health problems. Prison is no place for young people with mental health problems. The risk of suicide is all too evident with frequent reports of suicide in young offenders' institutions. Even the most progressive regimes are inadequate to the task of meeting these already damaged individuals' needs for stability, certainty, care, and proper support to tackle their offending behaviour within a context of restorative justice and personal responsibility, backed up by therapeutic input.

Looked after children

Nearly 60,000 children were being looked after by local authorities for the year ending 2001. About 60 per cent of these children had been abused or neglected with a further 10 per cent coming from 'dysfunctional families' (DoH, 2001). Abuse of this nature can lead to self-harming behaviour, severe behavioural problems and depression. Evidence confirms that the mental health needs of these children and young people are overlooked and that many have established mental health problems prior to coming into local authority care (Dimigen et al., 1999). 38,400 of these children were in foster placements and 6,400 were in children's homes, yet foster carers and residential staff are among the least qualified and supported people left to manage sometimes extreme behaviour. Specialist CAMHS services often decline to help because of the uncertain and possibly temporary nature of the child's placement which contra-indicates successful intervention. The dilemma is that without input, placements often break down as carers cannot cope, invariably leading to more placements and further deterioration in the child's mental health.

A recent research study emphasised the importance of a preventive approach with children in the public care system who are more likely to be excluded from school following emotional and behavioural difficulties (Fletcher-Campbell, 2001). Teacher training that fails to adequately prepare newly-qualified staff to respond to the mental health needs of pupils is considered to be a factor in the increased use of school exclusions (OFSTED, 1996). Social workers using a preventive approach could be helpful to teaching staff and organise collaborative work aimed at preventing difficult behaviour escalating. Unless the mental health needs of these children and young people are addressed as part of a strategy that effectively nurtures children's inclusion in school the risk of deterioration is high. The risk factors for looked after children are probably the most extreme of any socially excluded group, they include (Richardson and Joughin, 2000):

- developmental delay
- school failure
- communication difficulty
- low self esteem
- parent/carer conflict

- family breakdown
- rejection
- abuse
- parental mental illness
- alcohol/drug abuse
- poverty
- homelessness
- loss

Children with HIV/Aids

The stress experienced by children and families infected with HIV is magnified by societal attitudes and prejudice about HIV/Aids, and is a risk factor for the development of mental health problems in children and adolescents. These are some of the psycho-social stressors that can contribute towards the social exclusion of these vulnerable families (Boyd-Franklin et al., 1995):

- **Stigma and fear of contagion** – this can produce alienation and rejection by peers of children with HIV/AIDS. Parents can lose employment or become homeless as a result of perceived risks.
- **Shame, guilt and anger** – the stigma can produce intense feelings of shame, guilt and anger which are difficult to manage within the family system. Professionals may also blame drug abusing parents for causing their child's illness, further reinforcing feelings of despair.
- **Secrecy and social isolation** – families often live in secrecy with their diagnosis and the associated stigma of homosexuality, drug abuse or prostitution. The consequent social isolation and rejection from extended family support systems can trigger depression, suicidal thoughts, and poor compliance with medical care.

Denial and fleeing medical facilities are not uncommon responses to a positive diagnosis particularly among adults with alcohol or other substance abuse habits. The emotional shock following a period of denial may be characterised by intense feelings of hysteria and anger followed by depressive symptoms, withdrawal and feelings of shame and guilt. Unless these feelings are managed and contained in a helping relationship they will affect the emotional temperature in the household and pose a further risk to the mental health of children in the family. Social workers need to bear in mind that a simple referral about a child with emerging mental health problems could involve a child in the centre of an emotional whirlwind where the underlying cause cannot be revealed.

Working with HIV infected children requires similar skills to working with any child or adolescent with added emphasis on issues of trust, time, loss, secrecy and bereavement. Understanding the child's conception of the illness is a crucial task. This can build on what the child or young person already understands about chronic illness causality in general. The key is in adapting knowledge and information to the developmental level the child is at in order for effective communication to take place. An important and difficult issue is the decision about whether and when to disclose the diagnosis to the child. Conflicts between family members and professionals can take place over this most sensitive issue, and affect the emotional state of the child. These principles are generally followed (Pollock and Boland, 1990):

- The truth is generally less threatening to a child than fear of the unknown.
- Information needs to be presented at a level that is developmentally appropriate for the child.
- Disclosure is a process not an event.

Refugee and asylum seeking children

The number of applications for asylum from unaccompanied under 18s almost trebled between 1997 and 2001 from 1,105 to 3,469. DoH figures indicate that there were 6,750 unaccompanied asylum-seeking children supported by local authorities in 2001. Further evidence shows that many of these young people were accommodated and receiving a worse service than other children in need (Audit Commission, 2000). Very little research has been done to ascertain the mental health needs of this group of children. However there is some evidence of the symptoms of post traumatic stress syndrome being present before they then experience the racist xenophobic abuse of individuals and institutions incapable of demonstrating humanitarian concern for their plight. This combination can shatter the most psychologically robust personality. It has been estimated that serious mental health disorders may be present in 40–50 per cent of young refugees (Hodes, 1998).

The impact on the organisation and functioning of refugee and asylum seeking families is regarded as a risk factor for the development of mental health problems in children and young people. The children of torture victims may present with high levels of emotional and anxiety states even though they themselves have not been directly exposed to these traumatic events. Similarly, while children may adapt more easily to their new environment and develop language skills, their parents may not. This can cause inter-generational tension and lead to a reduction in parental influence and authority that becomes problematic at important developmental transition points such as adolescence (Hodes, 2000).

Roma, Gypsy and Traveller children may be included in recent groups of asylum and refugee seeking families escaping ethnic 'cleansing' from the Balkan region of Central and Eastern Europe. These children and families have a long history of persecution and flight from discrimination. Roma, Gypsy and Traveller families who have for many years made their home in Britain are probably one of the most socially excluded groups of people living in Britain. Unemployment among

Roma/Gypsies is in the region of 70 per cent, while increasing numbers of children are failing to complete even a basic education (Save the Children, 2001). These factors-particularly the lack of proper education, are risk factors for the development of mental health problems. The overall context of social exclusion means an absence of contact with preventive services or the positive interaction with peers necessary for developmental attainment.

Community practice and social development

The idea of community social work is based on the premise that most people's problems are sorted out within and between their existing local network of friends, relatives and neighbours. Social work has a role in seeking to reinforce and support those networks or helping to facilitate their growth where they have declined, as a protective and preventive child and adolescent mental health strategy. Community practice therefore is *par excellence* the optimum intervention strategy for promoting social inclusion. It does not as is sometimes assumed, exclude work with individuals. The spectrum of activity includes (Smale et al., 2000):

- **Direct intervention** – work carried out with individuals, families and local networks to tackle problems that directly affect them.
- **Indirect intervention** – work with community groups and other professionals and agencies to tackle problems affecting a range of people.
- **Change agent activity** – this seeks to change ways that people relate to each other that are responsible for social problems whether at individual, family or neighbourhood levels by reallocating resources.
- **Service delivery activity** – providing services that help to maintain people in their own homes, to reduce risks to vulnerable people, and provide relief to parent/carers.

Community practice is not just about transforming neighbourhoods whether in small or large scale but it can also enable personal change and growth in individuals through social action and the fostering of co-operative activity. The reverse of course is also true. Individual work such as that described earlier in this book that focuses on the internal mental health problems of children and families can also contribute to wider social transformation in neighbourhoods. Defining precisely what community social work is can be difficult, it can mean almost what anyone wants it to mean from visiting lonely housebound people to organising a protest march to the Town Hall to lobby for improvements to neighbourhood services (Thompson, 2002; Adams et al., 2002).

With such broad definitional parameters it is not surprising to conclude that there is a shortage of reliable empirical data about social work activity in this area of practice (Macdonald, 1999). The available evidence does suggest, however, that in the context of child and adolescent mental health, it is community-oriented, pro-active initiatives that are helping. Measurable improvements in specific areas such as parenting skills and general reductions in child mental health problems have been identified (Hutchings et al., 1998; Davis and Spurr, 1998; Walker, 2002). A modern, psycho-social model offers the appropriate holistic perspective for social workers to engage with other professionals in the community, to work in partnership with families, and employ the personal relationship skills the majority aspire to use. In a report to the United Nations world summit on social development the Save the Children Fund highlighted six problems in current planning for children that inhibits appropriate child-centred practice (Save the Children Fund, 1995):

- A failure to collect child specific information.
- Lack of recognition of children's productive contribution.
- No participation of children in decision-making.
- The use of an inappropriate 'standard model of childhood'.
- The pursuit of adult interests in ways which render children passive.
- Lack of attention to gender and generational relationships.

Anti-discriminatory practice

In Chapter 4 culturally competent practice in child and adolescent mental health work focused on highlighting the need to incorporate anti-racist principles with black children. Anti-discriminatory practice is a broader element of a socially inclusive practice that addresses the needs of those citizens who are prohibited from participating in the full services and resources available in society and families. It has been argued historically in social work that those classic theoretical practice models mentioned in earlier chapters have rarely sat easily with the concept of anti-discriminatory practice – they essentially reflect the existing power relationships dominated by white, middle class, heterosexual, male, healthy, employed, Westerners. However, these models can be updated, adapted, and used creatively rather than be rejected, so that their underlying strengths can be employed in a modern context. Some of the features of anti-discriminatory practice are (Thompson 2001):

- Work collaboratively.
- View users as competent.
- Help users to see themselves as having some strength.
- Develop their confidence by affirming their experiences.
- Help them seek diverse solutions.
- Help users build and use informal networks to increase access to resources.

The use and abuse of power is at the centre of anti-discriminatory practice. It is a significant element in every relationship but is not necessarily negative. Rather than becoming monitors of sexism, racism, disablism, or homophobia, it is more useful to think in terms of ensuring that social work clients have access to equal opportunities in the service provider environment and in the assessment and intervention plan formulated. To practice in an anti-discriminatory way means seeking to bridge the gap between social worker and service user in order to facilitate a negotiation of perceptions. This dialogic process is at the heart of a socially inclusive practice. It also fits with social workers desire to practice using the interpersonal relationship skills that they value most highly.

Gender is central to power issues and as workers or clients men need to be made aware in every situation of their potential to oppress, how maleness affects their perception of problems, and to be oppressed because of assumptions about masculinity. There is also increasing evidence that promoting and encouraging fathers' greater involvement in child care can enhance outcomes for children especially in terms of psycho-social development (Kraemer, 1995; Burghes et al., 1997). Social workers have an opportunity to engage with men at both these levels for the benefit of child and adolescent mental health. Lone fathers, men who are the main carers, or fathers who choose to share child care are to some extent socially excluded from community resources traditionally oriented towards women (Ghate et al., 2000).

Those very preventive resources such as family centres where much valuable work is done to prevent mental health problems becoming entrenched in vulnerable children are not accessible to men. A recent research study concluded that these centres needed to think about whether and how they might enable the attendance of fathers who were key to the emotional development of their children (Ghate et al., 2000). While some centres are implicitly refuges for many women who have been oppressed by men, their commitment to children's development requires them to consider the crucial role fathers play in that and how to facilitate contact. Social workers with a psycho-social perspective can combine the internal developmental needs of the child with the external social context of patriarchal and masculine power to ensure optimum mental health with physical and emotional safety.

Feminist social work practice engages both the personal and the social by focusing on the whole person and examining the inter-connectedness between people and the structures they live within. It provides a powerful explanatory tool to use in assessing situations involving child abuse and domestic violence. In terms of child and adolescent mental health problems it highlights the gender dimension to the multi-faceted assessment of problems and ways to support children and young people who are suffering. It may not be as simple as matching the gender of worker and service user either.

It may be therapeutically beneficial for a different gender worker to be helping a child or young person through traumatic feelings or the consequences of previous abusive experiences. The important point is that gender is considered alongside and equal in importance to, all other variables in the issues to be addressed.

Advocacy and partnership practice

Advocacy is associated with a rights-based socially inclusive approach to planning intervention and arises from a recognition that social work has not always empowered service users. It is at its simplest about speaking up for or acting on behalf of another person. The aim of advocacy is to make sure the client's voice is heard, to make sure the person gets the services they need, and to make sure the client knows their rights so they can work towards getting what they are entitled to (Bateman, 2000). One of the difficulties in applying this approach to children and adolescents with mental health problems is judging who the client is. A parent or carer may refer a child or young person for help but it may be that during the process of work with the child an assessment of their needs indicates the need for an advocacy approach. Being open, flexible, and using negotiation skills while receiving good quality supervision/consultation will help. Key principles informing advocacy practice are:

- The service user's voice and views are paramount.
- Good advocacy leaves the person more able to do it themselves.
- Advocacy should help people to make informed choices.
- Ensure the user feels in control of the process and trusts the advocate.
- Advise, assist and support – not pressurising or persuading.
- Always act in the client's best interest.
- Always act in accordance with the client's wishes and instructions.
- Keep the client properly informed.
- Carry out instructions with diligence and competence.
- Act impartially and offer frank, independent advice.
- Maintain rules of confidentiality.

It is important to make the distinction between the role of care manager and advocate. The social worker as care manager may be intervening for the needs of the service user in negotiations about services to be provided, but they have also to make judgements about what they think is needed in the client's best interests. Direct Payments are an example where budgets can be controlled by service users to select provision, but a social worker still assesses need and makes a judgement about the ability of a person to manage that budget. An advocate on the other hand can maintain their focus on representing the views of the client. There are three main types of advocacy:

Citizen advocacy – works on a one to one basis where usually volunteers act on behalf of those who require services. The citizen advocate primarily performs an instrumental role that can focus on welfare benefits problems or negotiating a care plan. There is also an expressive role that involves meeting emotional needs, befriending and providing support. This could be helpful with children and young people who wish to challenge enforced treatment decisions.

Self advocacy – involves training and group support to help people learn skills and gain emotional strength to advocate for themselves. It is also about personal and political needs focusing on participation in all areas of service planning and delivery. The aim is not just to improve services but to improve the status of service users. Self advocacy has the important function of facilitating collective action as well as making it easier for individuals to be assertive. This could be a valuable intervention within a community network of children and young people who find it hard to access conventional CAMHS services.

Group advocacy – brings people together with similar interests, so that they can operate as a group to represent their shared interests. Similar to self advocacy, the aim is to influence service delivery decisions and to reframe how certain problems or groups of clients are perceived by professionals. Group advocacy may be part of campaigning organisations operating in the voluntary sector. Adults with learning difficulties and mental health problems have been in the forefront of group advocacy as they have responded to depersonalised and institutional services failing to meet their needs. Child and adolescent mental health services need social workers to energise this particular strategy.

It is important to make distinctions about the different levels of partnership possible in a socially inclusive intervention. The assessing social worker rarely meets with an individual child or parent/carer on a truly voluntary basis therefore the experience is characterised by unequal power relations with decisions requiring professional judgement. Previous negative contact or the characteristics of the referral will influence perceptions between client and worker. However it is crucial to differentiate between making a judgement and being judgemental. The former requires facing up to the challenge of responsibility in order to be helpful, while the latter involves prejudice, blaming, and a closed mind (Trevithick, 2000).

Partnership practice has become embedded along with empowerment in social work practice guidance to the extent that there is little debate about whether this is always an appropriate strategy and whether service users have said they desire this approach. Partnership is normally thought of as a process where the key stakeholders in a service co-operate in defining how the service should be designed and delivered. This can happen in an individual or an organisational context. Parents may negotiate with a service for the best course of action to take in the interests of their child. Or young people who use services may represent other service users' opinions in an organisational forum. On the other hand both parent/carers and children may be quite disconcerted by talk of partnership working.

Research by Barnardo's concluded that of the parents who used their services none came with the intention of becoming a partner. Staff interviewed saw partnership as a strategy to empower users and build services around their views. Users on the other hand, saw partnership embodied in the friendliness, accessibility and helpfulness of staff (Daines et al., 1990). Other research highlights the challenges in working in partnership with absent parents of children in long term care many of whom may suffer emotional and behavioural problems. In these situations social workers have to contribute to planning on the basis of several conflicting issues and make a judgement about the viability of a partnership approach and how far to risk further harm to the child:

- The importance of promoting contact with parents, relatives, community and culture.
- The failings of the care system to enable children to reach their potential and fully meet their needs.
- The importance of birth families and the value of different attachments in helping children form their identity.
- In conflict-laden situations inadequate resources, inaccurate information, or changes of social worker have often passively hindered parents.
- The potentially destructive effects of persistent abandonment, rejection or neglect from a parent failing to maintain arranged contact.

One means of working in partnership is by *conferring* rights such as the approach adopted by the disability movement and which is often linked to discussions about citizenship. This is further defined as *participation* and has been summarised by Mullender and Ward (1991):

- All people have skills, understanding and ability.
- People have rights to be heard, to participate, to choose, to define problems and action.
- People's problems are complex and social oppression is a contributory factor.
- People acting collectively are powerful.
- Methods of work must be non-elitist and non-oppressive.

Case illustration

A pattern of referrals has been noticed in recent months during the warmer weather of children and young people congregating in well-known meeting places for disaffected youth on a notorious council estate. Several children are known to be missing school or have just left statutory secondary education. Reports of minor drug and alcohol use are regularly made as well as anxious calls to the police from older citizens following intimidatory encounters. There have been a few reports of vandalism and attempted burglaries. Teachers, the police, and GPs have asked for something to be done. Some young people known to your team are believed to be involved, and some basic research shows that there are some background issues suggestive of emerging mental health problems. *How might you intervene in a way consistent with a socially inclusive perspective?*

Commentary

Collecting and sharing information with other professionals is a good basis for planning how to respond in a collective and co-ordinated way. A meeting needs to be convened initially to test the commitment of key staff and to see what lines of communication exist or need to be created with the young people. Make sure children and young people have a say in the design, delivery and evaluation of supportive services. What is the evidence their contribution is valued, and what helps or hinders advocacy?

Making contact with everyone connected to the problem either plaintiff or defendant and facilitating expression of problem definition and proposed solutions. This can expose gaps in people's beliefs as well as areas for potential agreement. There may be little grounds for optimism and much scepticism, but an agenda can at least be constructed, even one with contradictions, confusions and incoherence.

The example of family group conferences involving as many people from a child's family being brought together to try to find solutions to child care/protection problems, offers some evidence for an effective way forward. Such a model could help facilitate bringing people together in a way that is rooted in service users own experience and resources (Morris and Tunnard, 1996). A grand vision of communal activity with streamlined organisational structures may be too ambitious but small incremental changes that have widespread support from those with antagonistic relationships may succeed where conventional service-led practice fails.

Groupwork and community work skills are indicated in such a project. They do not require wholesale transformation of social work practices but the application of core values and skills in a wider context. Networking, liaison, and joint working between different agencies with agreed aims and objectives are likely to produce success, rather than retraction behind agency boundaries and a retreat to the blame culture so prevalent in situations which seem hopeless. Lobbying for structural improvements and facilities via petitions or media exposure can make a big impact as a preventive strategy with very little effort.

A variety of resources needs to be available to enable the widest possible choice to be given to the children and young people able to engage with such a development. Depending on the level of need and capacity of individuals these could range from low-key youth activities, to specific groupwork addressing drug abuse, and individual counselling and therapeutic work around behaviour control and anxiety management for example.

Building a socially inclusive practice

Social workers have to assess needs, evaluate risks and allocate resources in a way that is equitable as far as possible for a wide range of children and adolescents in various situations. Challenging oppression in relation to key issues such as poverty and social marginalisation that underpin interactions in social welfare requires a holistic approach to social change that tackles oppression at the personal, institutional and cultural levels (Dominelli, 2002). Government social policy since the seventies has had a debilitating impact on state welfare services and in the process a new role has been devised for statutory social work, not so much as a provider of services or even as a therapeutic intervention but rather as a front-line service focused on the management of exclusion and rationing of scarce resources (Jones, 1997).

An empowering social work practice rejects this prescription. A review of the elements that constitute a socially inclusive practice lists four core intervention skills necessary to build on an authentic social work practice (Smale et al., 2000):

- social entrepreneurship
- reflection
- challenging
- reframing

Social entrepreneurship is the ability to initiate, lead and carry through problem-solving strategies in collaboration with other people in all kinds of social networks. Reflection is the worker's ability to pattern or make sense of information, in whatever form, including the impact of her/his own behaviour and that of the organisation on others. Challenging refers to the ability of staff to confront people effectively with their responsibilities, their problem-perpetuating/creating behaviours and their conflicting interests. Reframing is the worker's ability to help redefine circumstances in ways which lead towards problem resolution.

Social workers must counteract oppression, mobilise users' rights and promote choice, yet act within organisational and legal structures which users experience as oppressive (Braye and Preston-Shoot, 1997). Finding their way through this dilemma and reaching compromises, or discovering the potential for creative thinking and practice are the challenges and opportunities open to social workers committed to a socially inclusive practice. This means treating people as wholes, and as being in interaction with their environment, of respecting their understanding and interpretation of their experience, and seeing clients at the centre of what workers are doing (Payne, 1997). The unique psycho-social perspective of social work offers a vast reservoir of knowledge and skills to bring to bear on the mental health problems of socially excluded children and adolescents.

Summary of key points

Social workers are among those in the front line faced with the consequences of the failure of social policy aimed to reduce social exclusion and the raised expectations of people in need. There are disproportionate effects on the mental health of socially excluded children and young people. One in ten children in the United Kingdom suffers from a poverty related mental health problem and the UK is fourth from the bottom of a list of relative poverty among the nineteen richest nations.

Social work has a role in seeking to reinforce and support those community networks or helping to facilitate their growth where they have declined, as a protective and preventive child and adolescent mental health strategy. Community practice therefore is *par excellence* the optimum intervention strategy for promoting social inclusion. It does not as is sometimes assumed, exclude work with individuals.

Anti-discriminatory practice is a broader element of a socially inclusive practice that addresses the needs of those citizens who are prohibited from participating in the full services and resources available in society. To practice in an anti-discriminatory way means seeking to bridge the gap between social worker and service user in order to facilitate a negotiation of perceptions. This dialogic process is at the heart of a socially inclusive practice. It also fits with social workers desire to practice using the interpersonal relationship skills that they value most highly.

Some of the most socially excluded children and those whose mental health needs are to a large extent ignored, include black children, refugee and asylum seeking children, children with HIV/AIDS, disabled children, looked after children, and young offenders. Advocacy is associated with a rights-based socially inclusive approach to planning intervention for these young people. It is at its simplest about speaking up for or acting on behalf of another person.

Challenging oppression in relation to key issues such as poverty, social exclusion and the marginalisation that underpin interactions in social welfare requires a holistic approach to social change that tackles oppression at the personal, institutional and cultural levels. Social workers have an opportunity to put into practice their beliefs about social justice and equality combined with their concern for the mental health of vulnerable children and adolescents in a socially inclusive practice.

CHAPTER 8

Effectiveness and Evaluation

Introduction

There is as yet no substantial evidence base for effectiveness in services for children and adolescents with mental health problems. One of the few contemporary attempts to collate the available methodologically robust research emphasises the importance of specifying what intervention works for which families with what problems (Carr, 2000).

This is not an easy task. Evaluating provision in child and adolescent mental health services is particularly challenging because of the difficulty in isolating any factor which can be clearly demonstrated to have affected outcome (Target and Fonagy, 1996; Hunter et al., 1996; Audit Commission, 1999). The wide range of professionals from many agencies having some impact on child mental health is so diverse as to make it unrealistic to identify a linear sequence of causality from intervention through to outcome. There are just so many informal, psycho-social influences affecting children's emotional and behavioural development in the short term or cumulatively over the long term.

A review of the literature on empirical evaluations of family support services yielded mixed results and acknowledged that natural, developmental changes have the potential to be mistakenly attributed to effects due to the service (Rossi, 1992). Other research suggests that family support programmes in particular, tend to focus on a single outcome as a measure of success such as changes in a child's behaviour. Taking into account other dimensions such as improved parent/child interactions or better use of community resources could be more useful (Gardner, 1998; Franklin and Madge, 2000). Table 8.1 provides a guide to enable consideration of the range of approaches for particular problems that have shown effectiveness. These are intended as a broad guide only bearing in mind that every individual child requires support that feels right for them in their unique circumstances. Combinations of the approaches indicated may in some circumstances be more effective.

Effectiveness studies have tended to neglect the views of service users and especially children as independent evaluators (Sanford et al., 1992; Kent and Read, 1998; Laws et al., 1999). Equally, in studies attempting to validate service user evaluation a trend towards positive bias has been identified particularly where treatment is continuing (Polowczyk, 1993).

Social workers seeking to measure or gauge the impact of their work with children and adolescents in the area of mental health face a difficult challenge

Table 8.1: Mental health problems and possible interventions (Graham, 1996; Child Psychotherapy Trust, 1998; Carr, 2000)

Mental health problem	Intervention
Aorexia/bulimia nervosa	Family therapy, psychotherapy, cognitive-behaviour therapy
Anxiety	Counselling, school based group work, behaviour therapy, family therapy
Enuresis/encopresis	Behaviour therapy
School refusal	Behaviour therapy
Obsessional disorder	Medication, cognitive-behaviour therapy
Reading difficulties	Psychotherapy, counselling
Depression/grief	Psychotherapy, counselling, cognitive-behaviour therapy, family therapy
Diabetes control	Psychotherapy/counselling
Child abuse	Individual or group therapy, parent training
Conduct disorder/ aggression	Cognitive-behaviour therapy, family therapy, parent training, foster care
ADHD	Social skills training, family therapy, parent training, behaviour therapy
Adjustment to divorce/separation	Counselling, problem-solving training, social skills training
Oppositional defiant disorder	Parent training, behaviour therapy, group work, problem-solving training
Drug abuse	Family therapy, problem solving training, social skills training

particularly in the context of the drive to evidence-based practice. Traditional scientific research based methods are beyond the capacity of field social workers who are just about managing their caseloads and the day-to-day administration involved. Even some of the most well-resourced mental health professionals with time and advanced research skills cannot lay claim to levels of efficacy when there are so many variables affecting the outcomes for children and young people. The traditional randomised control trial may not provide a comprehensive assessment of outcome or represent accurately what actually happens in practice (Barnes et al., 1997; Barton, 1999). However, social workers can incorporate the concepts of effectiveness and evaluation in ways consistent with their professional ethics and values and in the best interests of their clients and by adopting a children's rights perspective.

Table 8.2: Health of the Nation (HoNOSCA) Scales (Gowers et al., 2000)

Scale item	Section
	Behaviour
Disruptive/aggressive behaviour	
Overactivity and attentional difficulty	
Non accidental self-injury	
Alcohol, substance/solvent misuse	
	Impairment
Scholastic or language skills	
Physical illness/disability problems	
Hallucinations and delusions	
Non organic and somatic symptoms	
Emotional and related symptoms	
	Social
Peer relationships	
Self-care and relationships	
Family life and relationships	
Poor school attendance	
	Information
Lack of knowledge-nature of difficulties	
Lack of information-services/management	

Each scale item scored in range 0–4.

Effectiveness

Quantitative measures that examine changes in symptoms that caused the initial concern are commonly used to evaluate outcome in child and adolescent mental health services. A particular set of measures is now being put into practice that was originally designed for adult mental health (Gowers et al., 1999, 2000). The items measured are classified into sections and a severity index is calculated for before and after comparison. Table 8.2 provides an indication of the items measured.

In-patient and day patient units are the intervention prescribed for some of the most disturbed young people, or whose development is being hampered significantly by family circumstances, or who have life threatening problems. There are very few reliable studies that have examined the outcome of these interventions because they are all different in size and type of client population. Social workers will more likely be interested in qualitative measures that address questions to do with:

- How a child or young person is functioning in their social environment.
- Gaining their accounts of what they define as success.
- Whether they can get on better with mates.
- Do they feel more able to cope with stress?

The literature on effectiveness tends to focus on evaluating specific service interventions but it should be acknowledged that broader fiscal and social policies impact on children and their families and therefore contribute-for good or bad to the context of children's welfare overall (Holterman, 1995). It has long been assumed that early intervention is the key to effectiveness because it stops problems getting worse before they become harder and more costly to tackle. It also reduces damage to children's development, family relationships, use of scarce resources, and prevention of anti-social consequences in the long-term (Bayley, 1999). However, it has been pointed out that the accumulated evidence for the effectiveness of early intervention programmes is not as optimistic as was once hoped (Eayrs and Jones, 1992). On occasion there is the possibility that such programmes can be damaging, de-skilling, and undermining of parents confidence.

On the other hand a meta-analysis of early education interventions demonstrates that children from disadvantaged backgrounds were less at risk from developing maladjustment, school failure and delinquency after participating in the programmes. Outcome research on primary prevention mental health programmes focussed on school-based activities concluded that positive changes occurred in social adjustment, academic performance, and cognitive skills leading to a reduction in mental health problems (Sylva, 1994; Durlak, 1998). The location of child and adolescent mental health services is therefore critical in engaging parents and children. Schools are emerging as an acceptable and accessible non-stigmatising venue for individual or group-based activity.

Research on the effectiveness of individual therapies for children has lagged far behind that on treatment for adults, just as the development of assessment measures of childhood functioning has been much slower. A comprehensive review of psychotherapy research demonstrated that often adult treatments are inappropriately adopted for children, but meta-analyses demonstrate that broadly speaking, therapy seems to be better than no therapy (Roth and Fonagy, 1996). Behavioural and cognitive-behavioural treatment appears to be more effective used individually or in family approaches than psycho-dynamic approaches, but there are problems in comparing data and the limited history of rigorous evaluation particularly when concurrent treatments for individuals and other family members are offered. Recent meta-analyses of family therapy demonstrate effectiveness with specific problems such as adolescent substance abuse, and anorexia nervosa (Stanton and Shadish, 1997).

A major review of consumer studies of family therapy and marital counselling analysed a variety of research including large and small scale studies, individual case studies, specific therapeutic methodologies and ethnographic studies (Treacher, 1995). It concluded that practitioners who neglected the service user perspective and undervalued the personal relationship aspects of their family support work in favour of concentrating on inducing change, ran the risk of creating considerable dissatisfaction among service users. This reinforced findings from an earlier study into the effectiveness of family therapy that advised that advice and directive work needs to be balanced with reflective and general supportive elements (Howe, 1989).

It is also important to take account of the natural history and environmental context of children's problems in relation to their developmental stage and acknowledge that there are no standardised ways of measuring childhood functioning. As discussed earlier many of these classic measures are based on white Eurocentric models that are not nowadays consistent with culturally competent practice. What is consistent in all the major studies is the general absence and rarity of service user evaluation of, and involvement in, the design of child and adolescent mental health research. The implication is that by enlarging the focus of effectiveness measures it is possible to see children not just with problems but also as having positive and constructive elements in their family lives and building on these and amplifying them wherever possible. They also have much to tell us about how they feel about research into their lives and how methodologies can become more child-centred.

This view is echoed in recommendations based on thorough research into interventions targeted at the child, teacher and parent which demonstrate that the combined effect produces the most sustained reduction in conflict problems, both at home and at school, and in peer relationships (Webster-Stratton, 1997). Recognising and building on the children's own perspectives provides new opportunities for social work with children and families guided by possibilities adults are not aware of or fail to pay enough attention to.

Service user evaluation

Taking the service user perspective into account in determining effectiveness has become a feature of contemporary policy in Social and Health care contexts but practice evidence does not support the policy aspiration (Kelson, 1997; Crawford and Kessel, 1999; Barnes and Warren, 1999). Also in seeking to evaluate one particular aspect of child and adolescent mental health service provision such as family support, it is problematic to define who the service user is. One of the challenges in defining effectiveness in family support interventions is clarifying for whom is it effective? Family support usually means mother support as fathers' absence is a feature of the helping context despite efforts to engage men in programmes to effect change.

There is evidence of activity to engage men in work but what little that has been undertaken has rarely been subject to rigorous evaluation (Holt, 1998). Mothers' evaluation of support may differ in more or less ways than the evaluation of the child or father irrespective of whether the focus of intervention was on an individual child, adult couple, or the whole family. A school-based behavioural problem may be resolved but at the expense of a deterioration in the parent/child relationship. A community focused intervention that aims to introduce change into the overall social environment may achieve short-term success in reducing anti-social activity, but unless it is supported and sustained over a longer time period the situation could deteriorate. An initial evaluation therefore might look positive but a longitudinal study could appear quite negative. Robust methods of differential evaluation by all participants, referrers, users and providers, would enhance the sophistication of the current data on effectiveness.

The House of Commons Health Committee recently reported that services for children and young people do not always focus on their needs. And a survey conducted by the SSI to examine the development of Children's Service Plans identified gaps in planning structures and relationships, one of which was the virtual absence of users from the planning process (HMSO, 1997, 1998). Similar findings have been reported with respect to NHS service development (Debell and Everett, 1997; Lansdowne, 1995). There is evidence that research into children's perceptions as recipients of helping services that focuses on competence and resources, rather than problems or deviance, helps provide a fuller picture of their circumstances and highlights the importance of the personal relationship established with their social worker or counsellor (Sandbaek, 1999). It is also consistent with the right under the terms of the UN Charter to be consulted with and to express their views about, services provided for them (UN, 1989).

Creating acceptable, accessible, and appropriate child and adolescent mental health services for every family that requires it, means acknowledging the poor general health of ethnic minority families attributable to their impoverished socio-economic circumstances and the impact of personal and institutional racism. Further research with ethnic minority families to investigate effectiveness is required to build on the limited work undertaken (Trevino, 1999). The needs of gay and lesbian families are virtually absent in the literature on family support which reflect homophobic and discriminatory practices in health and social care generally. This gap needs to be filled on the grounds of equality and to ensure appropriate support can be offered to every family however it is defined and to enable different parenting practices to be valued and learned from (Salmon and Hall, 1999; Eliason, 1996).

Children and young people as service evaluators

Effectiveness and evaluation in social work and to a much greater extent, in child and adolescent mental health services, has tended to be a service or professional-led enterprise. Managers and practitioners have developed methods and models of evaluating service provision using sophisticated research designs, methodologies, and computerised analysis to try to tell them something useful about the process and outcomes of their work. These can range from huge epidemiological studies to try to assess likely demand for certain services, through to micro studies of small organisational operations contemplating changes. The majority of these studies tend to be quantitative designs linked to clinical audit where service use is calculated against cost and efficiency measures such as length of client contact time. Evaluation is defined as making an assessment of the merit of an activity or intervention and measuring it against the goals that were established at the outset (Barlow et al., 2001). Quantitative approaches have been unfavourably compared to qualitative approaches because they lack the intensity, subtlety, particularity, ethical judgement and relevance required for example, by social workers (Shaw, 1999; May, 2002).

Children's perspectives and the qualitative information that articulates their agenda have rarely been explored in relation to the help they receive towards their emotional and mental wellbeing (Hill et al., 1995; Gordon and Grant, 1997). Findings that young people with mental health problems are reluctant to make use of specialist services or quickly cease contact indicates the importance of developing appropriate local sources of help (Mental Health Foundation, 1999; Audit Commission, 1999; Richardson and Joughin, 2000). It is crucial that children and young people are properly consulted to ensure that provision is experienced as useful and relevant and therefore going to be used effectively. In order to do that methods of consulting with children and young people need to be developed that are appropriate, effective and methodologically robust (Walker, 2001b).

There is a growing literature on the subject of the rights of children and young people to influence decisions about their own health and healthcare (MacFarlane and McPherson, 1995; Treseder, 1997; Wilson, 1999; Alderson, 2000). However, this remains an area of contention for some professionals who believe that the notion that children can think, comment, and participate in a meaningful way in evaluations of the help they receive, is at best misguided or at worst undermining parental or professional responsibility. There is perhaps added poignancy when this concept is applied to child and adolescent mental health, where the very emotional and behavioural problems of children give weight to the argument against seeking children's perceptions.

Parents and those with parental responsibility might present powerful arguments for wanting to make exclusive decisions to enable them to cope with and manage sometimes worrying and disturbing behaviour. Equally, where children's difficulties are located in the context of parental discord, abuse, domestic violence or family dynamics it is important to ensure children are not blamed or scapegoated for problems caused by events or actions outside their control (Cooper et al., 1999; Sutton, 1999; Dallos and Draper, 2000).

Research evidence demonstrates the value of consulting children and seeing how much they can achieve with a little help which is appropriate and acceptable (Levine, 1993; Griffiths, 1998). Children, like adults, have the right, under the terms of the UN Convention (Article 12) to be consulted with, and to express their views about, services provided for them (UN, 1989). In public services in England and Wales there is a legal duty to consult children in order to ascertain their wishes and feelings (Children Act 1989). Several studies provide some evidence of the effectiveness of attempts to ascertain the perceptions of children and young people about services they have received. There is among some practitioners and researchers a general assumption that seeking the views of children and young people is of itself a good thing. Yet the purpose of gaining such perceptions can be varied, the methods employed quite different, and the evidence of the impact of seeking their views, obscure.

A meta-review of these studies concluded that with the increasing interest in seeking children's views there need to be better developed instruments for measuring satisfaction and gaining children's evaluation of the services they receive (Hennessey, 1999). Research on children's evaluations of education, paediatrics, and child mental health services was assessed. Only a minority of studies examined had presented information on the structure, reliability, and validity of the instruments they used. Most of the studies concerned education contexts. The paediatric studies treated parents as the sole clients, while in mental health studies the correspondence between children's and parents evaluations of services seemed to be greater (Walker, 2001b).

Interviews and open-ended questions have the potential to provide valuable information on client evaluations that cannot be tapped by rating scales. Most studies presented limited information on the psychometric properties of the instruments used. Where information was presented it was limited to information on the internal consistency of the instrument used. Only a small number of studies presented any information on re-test reliability. Where the data were qualitative, researchers typically reported inter-rater reliability on the classification of the children's responses. Findings suggest it is possible to develop an instrument with good psychometric properties for use by children age six plus, there is however little evidence on instruments developed for use by younger children.

There is little literature about the best way to establish validity. Social workers know that the voice of the child is paramount and can easily agree with the view of a researcher who says that 'the criterion for validity is hard to derive from any source other than the child itself' (Tiller, 1988). Social workers may have used questionnaires in the context perhaps of groupwork or individual work where they were seeking to ascertain the wishes and feelings of children about their situation or the work that had been completed. The evidence suggests that not all questionnaire-based studies give information on how questionnaire items were selected for inclusion. Some are derived from consultation with experts or professional evaluators, teachers or day care staff, or adapted from those used with adult clients.

A small number of studies report that children were involved in the development of the questionnaires (Simonian et al. 1993; Shapiro et al. 1997). The conclusion is that poor attention to the issue of content validity has been paid. 'There is little evidence to suggest that the majority of questionnaires used to establish children's satisfaction with services actually addresses aspects of the service that are salient or relevant for their child clients.' (Hennessey, 1999). There is however, more evidence of better validity of satisfaction questionnaires from child mental health services. (Stuntzer-Gibson et al., 1995).

The extent to which children's evaluations are similar to the evaluations of parents raises important questions about validity. It can be assumed that perceptions should be different, but in the area of child and adolescent mental health differences in perception of the help received can indicate that the underlying cause of the difficulty remains untreated. The parents who want a child to conform and change her/his behaviour will have a different view of that child who wants them to stop arguing and fighting. In the case of a child this can result in symptom deterioration reinforcing parental perceptions that it is the child who has the problem. Such a consequence could lead to disillusionment and produce a resistance from the child at an older age to engaging with further help, thereby contributing to the development of mental health problems into adulthood.

It is important to explore the extent to which services are meeting the needs of differing groups of children in terms of age, gender, ethnicity, religion, and socio-economic status. The research on the relationship between client satisfactions in mental health services is better developed than in any other service sector. Three types of outcome have been used: client-assessed, parent-assessed, and therapist-assessed. There are inconsistent findings reported for the relationship between client satisfaction and therapist evaluation of treatment progress. The problem of practitioner power and status is regarded as influential in determining the ability of children and young people to express discontent with help offered. It is recognised that children and young people feel under pressure to say what they expect the practitioner to hear. Social workers in this context need to call upon their relationship-building skills and create an atmosphere of honesty and trust in order to obtain authentic feedback.

A few studies have looked at the relationship with personal and/or family variables. Understanding these relationships is potentially important for understanding the way in which services may or may not be meeting the needs of various clients. The information currently available is limited. There have been relatively small numbers of attempts to do this and those that have, used different measures. It is now acknowledged at central government level that children from different socio-economic backgrounds may have differential access to mental health services and different expectations from services, but to date these possibilities have not been further explored (Audit Commission, 1999).

Age is a particularly important variable because of the different cognitive, social and emotional needs and abilities of children of different ages. Although individual studies differed in whether younger or older clients were more satisfied, a sufficient number of studies reported a moderate or high correlation between age and satisfaction/dissatisfaction (Shapiro, 1997). Only a small number of studies explored the relationship between gender and satisfaction but the evidence suggests no general tendency for greater satisfaction to be associated with either boys or girls. A more useful approach may be to explore the relationship between client/staff gender combinations (Bernzweig et al., 1997).

There is very little evidence in many studies to demonstrate what impact their findings had on service development or practitioner attitudes and skills. A shift in thinking is required from perceiving children and young people as recipients of health promotion efforts on their behalf, to accepting children and young people as active participants in the whole process (Kalnins et al., 1992). Another gap in the literature is the limited information on how children and young people felt about being asked their views on the service that they had received. Some children may feel perturbed by this while others are enthusiastic about being given the opportunity to be part of a reflective process. It is a reasonable assumption that in the case of children and young people with mental health problems, those keenest to contribute are likely to reflect a positive perception of the service whereas those least keen reflect a negative experience. It is important for social workers and researchers to continue to develop creative and flexible methods for enabling representative contributions from all those receiving the same service.

Children's experience of help

Social workers have built up a repertoire of therapeutic methods in working with children and young people, engaging with them in areas of great sensitivity such as bereavement, parental separation, or sexual abuse. The same repertoire of research techniques is yet to be developed to ensure that children and young people are being given the best possible chance of contributing to service evaluation. Few studies have been undertaken with regard to therapeutic interventions with children and young people experiencing emotional and behavioural difficulties and whether they found the therapy helpful. Those undertaken have found generally children speak less than parents when interviewed together. Adolescents express themselves in limited ways tending to agree/disagree; while therapists spoke more often to parents than to children when attempting to evaluate the help and support offered (Marshal et al., 1989; Friedlander et al., 1985; Mas et al., 1985; Cederborg, 1997). The question is whether this reflects a generalisable aversion to participating in research of this nature or whether the research design militates against inclusion and active participation.

Children's reactions to therapy can be influenced by their attachment style. In families where there are insecure attachments for example, children can feel constrained to speak more freely because of fears of what the consequences might be and the discomfort in exposing painful or difficult feelings (Smith et al., 1996; Strickland-Clark et al., 2000). This poses important challenges for social workers and researchers wanting to gain feedback from children and young people with mental health problems where there are factors likely to inhibit participation. The alternative is to automatically exclude some children and young people and miss the opportunity to gather valuable evidence to improve service provision rather than designing strategies to overcome these difficulties. Ways to engage such children have been developed and could be adapted by researchers.

Therapeutic intervention can be usefully evaluated in terms of peoples' experiences of helpful versus unhelpful events (Llewlyn, 1988). Further significant aspects of these can be explored in a collaborative way by means of engaging with children and adolescents in evaluation using instruments such as the Comprehensive Process Analysis developed as a means of encouraging participation in exploring the experience of therapeutic intervention (Elliot and Shapiro, 1992). However, instruments such as this developed for use with adults need to be carefully considered for their suitability and appropriateness for use with children. There has been a tendency in approaches to facilitate communication with children to favour those that are standardised and produce quantifiable results (McGurk, 1992). There is a full literature about observational techniques for example, but little that addresses qualitative approaches. There is nevertheless, an emerging trend to move towards emphasising children's competencies and strengths in being able to describe their own perceptions (Williamson and Butler, 1996; Mayall, 1994).

There is little guidance available in the research literature about conversational methods with children. Even child psychology texts concentrate on experimental, observational and standard measurement techniques (Vasta, Haith and Miller, 1993). The perceived power and status of adults affect children in interview situations and by presumptions about what answers are expected. The combination of adult assumptions about children and young persons competence in contributing to service evaluation, together with children and young persons assumptions about adult power and authority, conspire to hinder meaningful developments to improve the situation.

Methodologies for including children

When efforts are made to overcome resistance to incorporating children and young persons' perceptions in service evaluation there is much evidence of creative and sensitive work being undertaken (Walker, 2001b). Several studies conclude that there are a number of factors that can help a practitioner in gaining confidence and the co-operation of young people, together with their perceptions and views (Finch, 1987; Pollard, 1987; Hazel, 1995; Hill et al., 1996). These are summarised below:

- **The fieldwork setting:** needs to achieve a balance between privacy needed for confidential data collection, and openness to public scrutiny for assuring the personal safety of the young person and minimise any risk of allegations of impropriety against the practitioner.
- **Vignettes:** of relevant social situations presented to a group of children for comment may be a particularly useful tool to use at the beginning of an interview to break the ice and encourage someone other than the practitioner to speak.
- **Short stories:** containing issues that might draw strong moral opinions, is likely to produce more confident information flow.
- **Pictures and photographs:** are effective ways of obtaining the full attention of young participants, demanding concentration of the eyes and mind. Having an object to handle can also be reassuring.
- **Free imagination and play:** young participants seem more enthusiastic and confident about telling their versions of events rather than commenting on vignettes created by the researcher. This encourages and corresponds to developmental level requiring characters or figures from their own sex.
- **Quotations or catch-phrases:** can be useful in encouraging strong opinions from children, these can be proverbs, or common sayings such as 'children should be seen and not heard'. Linked with popular culture drawn from media, especially TV soaps and news events, presentation of this material can provide successful sources of stimulation.
- **Problem solving:** children seem to draw comfort from their own knowledge and common ground held by the practitioner. Asking young people to propose a solution to a practical problem enables them to deal with problems involved in caring for people of their own or a younger age and enables the researcher to explore the reasons and more abstract beliefs behind the chosen solution. Presenting a problem in the style of a teenage magazine problem page may be a very accessible way of developing this technique.

It is important to continually reassure participants that there are no correct or incorrect responses to any issue that arise. Fear of false perceptions may be more likely in an educational setting where tests are a familiar occurrence. A mixture of focus group and individual interview techniques with children and adolescents on the subject of emotional and behavioural difficulties demonstrates an effective combination (Hill et al., 1996). Children begin by writing or drawing some basic information about themselves such as their likes or dislikes, favourite food, music, games or school subjects. This reinforces the point that the interviews are about their perceptions, not about getting the right answer. Each child can then be helped to complete an eco-map-a chart of people and places in their network that are important to them. The eco-map could be used with sentence completion cards to elicit actual examples or to explore who in practice children turn to in specific situations. It could also help ascertain which responses of other people in those situations were perceived as helpful or unhelpful. Simply asking what else could have been done or who else might have helped can produce important information. Role plays using psychodrama techniques can be used to bring alive situations and enhance the generation of meaningful information (Hill et al., 1996).

Focus group discussions have acquired prominence in recent years and their use with children can result in more information generated by individuals who are encouraged to voice their opinions when others do so. They seem able to develop their own points in response to the stimulation, challenge, and memory -prompting of what others say. There are individuals who do not find this format helpful, and it is important for the interviewer to facilitate productive peer interaction rather than create many individual interviews happening at the same time (Kitzinger, 1994). The optimum size of the group is recommended to be five to six, with a small age range, while some advocate single-sex groups (Greenbaum, 1987; Triseliotis et al., 1995).

It may be that gender differences at specific developmental stages can serve to accentuate different styles of expression, therefore thought needs to be put in to consider the optimum age range and gender mix of children. Another area with the potential to provide a rich source of information is in non-verbal communication. The advantage of developing methodologies for interpreting this level of communication is that it can enable access to much younger children's perceptions and those with disabilities, sensory impairments or developmental delays.

Ethical considerations

In seeking to ascertain the perceptions of children and young people about mental health services the primary ethical consideration is to prevent any harm or wrongdoing during the process of evaluation. While respecting children's competencies social workers need to also fulfil their responsibilities to protect children and young people. A more social-anthropological approach that allows data to be co-produced in the relationship between social worker and child, rather than being driven by problem-oriented adult questions is more appropriate because it permits the building up of information on the general topic over time.

There is considerable uncertainty about the issue of children's consent to participate in evaluative research. The issue has yet to be fully tested in court. This is linked to consent for treatment which has been affected by the decision of the

House of Lords in1985 (Gillick 3 All ER) ruling that competent children under 16 years of age can consent. Since then further court cases have modified the Gillick principle so that if either the child or any person with parental responsibility gives consent to treatment, doctors can proceed, even if one or more of these people, including the child, disagree. While these rulings do not strictly apply to evaluation they have implications for children's rights.

Parents may have to sign a research consent form until their child is 16 or 18 for medical research. But non-invasive social and educational evaluative research may not require parental consent because of the lack of harm. Social research requiring answers to questions implies consent if the subject co-operates. But is a child co-operating under pressure, afraid to decline or to challenge adult authority figures? It is argued that the onus should be on the adults to prove that the child does not have the capacity to decide, and the safest route is to ask for parental consent as well as the children's, when they are able to understand (Alderson, 1995). In the context of child and adolescent mental health the concept of informed consent requires sensitive explanation of the nature and purpose of evaluation clearly and unambiguously, and at the very least, allows informed dissent from the children and young people themselves (Morrow and Richards, 1996).

There is little evidence of researchers actively involving children to select topics, plan research or advise on monitoring research. Where this has been done the results demonstrate that young people value being asked to participate in this way, and have much to offer the development of the research process. It has been established that using teenagers as researchers with other young people, for instance, has certain advantages over using adult researchers (Alderson, 1995). Properly supported and trained they can engage with younger children in ways adults are unable to achieve. Social workers seeking more creative ways of evaluating service provision and keen to develop innovative services are ideally placed to facilitate this.

The timing of evaluation with children and young people with mental health problems, feedback to them, and the dissemination of findings, are further topics for ethical consideration. Attempting to interview during the course of intervention could be invasive or undermining of the therapeutic or supportive work being undertaken. Gaining access to children and young people after the problem has resolved could be hampered by a need for the child and family to put their experiences behind them and avoid being reminded of painful issues. Sending a questionnaire through the post is unlikely to elicit a response, and attempting to summarise a period of work during the final meeting might just not feel right.

Ethically the findings should be fed back to participants but in practice the time delay between data collection and writing up, together with access to children militate against achieving this aim. Dissemination of the findings and the use to which they are put by service managers or government departments presents a clear responsibility to social workers to ensure that the views and perceptions of the children and young people are not misrepresented or distorted. Children as a powerless group in society are usually not able to challenge the ways in which research findings about them are presented (Thomas and O'Kane, 1998).

Children's rights perspective

The language of children's needs permeates the professional literature, policy guidance and legislative frameworks that contextualise social work practice with children and young people. Replacing the concept of children's needs with that of children's rights offers a direct challenge to the paternalistic protectionist constructions that emphasise children as powerless dependents who are effectively excluded from participating in shaping their own environment. The idea that such provision is in the best interests of the child is a commonly used justification but quite meaningless. In child and adolescent mental health this means adopting a child's eye view of the world and enlisting them in designing more relevant needs assessment models and accessible support services. Interests like needs are not a quality of the child but a matter of cultural interpretation that is context-specific and open to multiple interpretations (Woodhead, 1997).

It has been argued that the increase in child and adolescent mental health problems over the last twenty-five years, is among other factors, the result of a lack of appropriate local people and places to which children and young people can turn (The Children's Centre, 1994). When they are suffering emotional pain or deeply troubled about something that is beyond them or their parent's capacity to resolve, a community approach is needed to help such children and young people which requires:

- Listening to children and treating them as people first and as clients second.
- Ensuring that children are informed fully about relevant actions and interventions and are allowed to inspect reports and records written about them.
- Consulting them about any significant decisions that will affect their lives, and involving them in the decision-making process.
- Taking what they say seriously and, whenever it seems necessary to act against their expressed wishes, explaining clearly why this has been decided and indicating how the child can challenge the decision.
- Knowing and ensuring that the child knows the rights which they do have, including the right to consent or withhold consent to medical treatment and the right to a legal representative of their own choice.
- Ensuring that they are aware of the channels for complaining about any aspect of their treatment or placement and in particular, ensuring that any incident which the child regards as wrong or unjust is investigated immediately and fully.

- Ensuring that if a child is sent in emergency to a placement which is known to be unsuitable and/or against their expressed wishes, there is an immediate review of the decision.
- Ensuring that if the child's liberty is restricted, they know their legal rights to challenge the detention, have access to experience and independent legal advice, and do not lose their entitlement to other rights.
- Being prepared to take seriously children's growing rights to self-determination and, in the interests of their welfare, for adults to take certain risks. All non-restrictive options should be considered carefully, before a decision is made to seek restriction of liberty.

Change and the practice evidence-base

Central to an empowering socially inclusive approach in social work with children and adolescents is finding out whether the work has contributed towards the process of change. Change can be considered as something that is endless, constant and inevitable. How it is perceived and experienced by service users is crucial. Various models of intervention permit change stemming from within the psyche of the person to physical changes in their environment and abilities. There are changes imposed on certain clients compulsorily and those that are accepted voluntarily- either of which may lead to long-term benefits for them or their kin. Change is often thought of as something initiated by a social worker in a linear cause and effect process. But it can be useful to think about it in a more circular or reflexive pattern. How much did the social worker change during the course of an intervention? What impact did the client have on them and how did this affect their thinking and behaviour? Indeed most of the change may occur within the social worker themselves as they find out more over time about a person and their circumstances compared to the first encounter.

Change is connected to difference but every stakeholder in the change process has a unique perception of what counts as difference. Pointing out differences to a person might be experienced as empowering but it might equally provoke feelings of fear or anxiety. A minimum amount of help might produce significant changes and equally a substantial amount of intervention results in no change or a worsening of circumstances. Where a social worker chooses to look for change may not be where other professionals or the service user is looking. Change can therefore be liberating or constraining, it can generate enlightenment or promote feelings of anger, loss and bereavement. Maintaining a degree of professional optimism with realism and managing uncertainty with a modest and respectful approach offers social workers the potential for being a useful resource to their clients.

Seven stages of change have been described which serve as a useful tool for social workers trying to evaluate their practice and assess the effectiveness of the chosen intervention with an individual child or young person (Rogers,1957). The stages can be used with the child or young person, or parent/carer, to include them in the process of insight development and self-reflection:

- **Stage 1:** Communication is about external events.
- **Stage 2:** Expression flows more freely.
- **Stage 3:** Describes personal reactions to external events.
- **Stage 4:** Descriptions of feelings and personal experiences.
- **Stage 5:** Present feelings are expressed.
- **Stage 6:** A flow of feeling which has a life of its own.
- **Stage 7:** A series of felt senses connecting different aspects of an issue.

The need to expand and refine the evidence base of social work practice in order to demonstrate effectiveness is more important than ever especially in work with children and adolescents with mental health problems. The growing problem requires a concerted effort from all agencies in contact with children and young people to understand the services they are providing and finding out better ways of measuring success. Three key factors have been identified in defining and explaining why evidence-based practice is not an option, but a necessity (Sheldon and Chilvers, 2000):

- **Conscientiousness** – this means a constant vigilance to monitor and review social work practice and to maintain service user welfare as paramount. It entails keeping up to date with new developments and a commitment to further professional understanding of human growth and development and social problems.
- **Explicitness** – this means working in an open and honest way with clients based on reliable evidence of what works and what is understood to be effective. The principle of explicitness demands a review of the available options with clients based upon thorough assessment of their problems.
- **Judiciousness** – this means the exercise of sound, prudent, sensible, judgement. Potential risks arising from some, or no intervention either in cases or policies, should be thoroughly assessed and evaluated in the knowledge that not all eventualities can be predicted.

The drive to encourage a research-minded profession in order to improve practice standards and accountability is however in danger of producing a confusion of research studies varying in quality and methodological rigour yet producing potentially useful data hidden within the quantity being produced. Practitioner research in social work is being encouraged as a means of influencing policy, management and practice using evaluative concepts moulded by service-user expectations (Fuller, 1996). In the context of child and adolescent mental health social workers can contribute to good quality effectiveness and evaluation studies by working in partnership with children and young people to ensure their perspectives are at the heart of this activity.

Summary of key points

Effectiveness and evaluation measures in child and adolescent mental health services have yet to develop a substantive evidence base to enable social workers to gauge what form of help and support is the right one for a particular child or young person at a particular time in particular circumstances.

The literature on effectiveness tends to focus on evaluating specific service interventions but it should be acknowledged that broader fiscal and social policies impact on children and their families and therefore contribute-for good or bad to the context of children's welfare overall. Early intervention is, generally, the key to effectiveness because it stops problems getting worse before they become harder and more costly to tackle.

Quantitative and qualitative data need to be combined in culturally competent ways in order to reflect the complexity of the circumstances of each individual child or young person being helped, and to incorporate their perception of the helping process. There is evidence that research into children's perceptions as recipients of helping services that focuses on competence and resources, rather than problems or deviance, helps provide a fuller picture of their circumstances and highlights the importance of the personal relationship established with their social worker or counsellor.

There is little evidence of researchers actively involving children to select topics, plan research or advise on monitoring research. Where this has been done the results demonstrate that young people value being asked to participate in this way, and have much to offer the development of the evaluation process. Children as a powerless group in society are usually not able to challenge the ways in which research findings about them are presented.

Change can be liberating or constraining, it can generate enlightenment or promote feelings of anger, loss and bereavement. Maintaining a degree of professional optimism with realism and managing uncertainty with a modest and respectful approach offers social workers the potential for being a useful resource to children and adolescents.

The need to expand and refine the evidence base of social work practice in order to demonstrate effectiveness is more important than ever especially in work with children and adolescents with mental health problems. The growing problem requires a concerted effort from all agencies in contact with children and young people to understand the services they are providing and finding out better ways of measuring success.

Conclusion

The greatest chance of positive change in children with conduct problems and emotional difficulties consistent with early signs of mental health problems lies mainly in improvements in their family circumstances, positive peer group relationships, and good school experiences, and less in direct contact with specialist child psychiatric services. (Rutter, 1991).

This is impressive advice from one of the most renowned and internationally acclaimed child psychiatrists. This is also my conclusion. Lack of appropriate provision is one of the key issues facing children and young people with mental health problems. A government inquiry discovered that more than a third of Health Trusts could not respond effectively to a young person in crisis; only half had proper procedures for emergency cover; and 10 per cent could not offer a non-urgent appointment within six months (Audit Commission, 1999). In some areas there are no specialist services at all whereas others are spending seven times more than the average.

There is no coherent national strategy for CAMHS. Children's mental health needs have to compete with other demands in the health care system and the Primary Care Trusts who are responsible for commissioning services are struggling to manage their role. Multi agency partnerships are meant to be the *modus operandi* of CAMHS but there are problems because of the different expectations from each partner agency of what CAMHS outcomes should be. Part of the problem with the organisation of CAMHS is whether to conceive it as a comprehensive or specialist service- in other words a preventive or reactive provision. A preventive focus requires a planned training and educational programme for primary care, social work, health, and education staff. Reactive provision is against universalist principles, is likely to be more costly in the long run and cannot contribute to health promotion.

The increasing trend towards including children and young people as active, rather than passive recipients of health and social care means that the task of developing robust methods for obtaining children and young peoples perceptions is important. Enabling them to collaborate in the design of research studies and to be consulted fully about the areas they consider important to research can only enrich these studies. The impact such research has in terms of the immediate effect on the child or young person, and on later service and practitioner development, are areas requiring attention from researchers involved in this area of work. This highlights the need for continued vigilance and effort by social workers in the area of children's rights.

The views of parents are largely absent from the research, particularly in lone parent families, gay and lesbian parents, and step parents. There is also very little systematic incorporation of culture and ethnicity as factors influencing parenting styles, on disability and the particular issues facing parents with disabled children who may have emotional and behavioural problems, and on gender influences within families and within professional groups. Further studies which pay attention to normative models of parenting in the community would counter this bias by identifying skills that lead to successful parenting- focusing on what went right rather than what went wrong. Anti-racist practice demands attention to the family life cycle/course of black and other ethnic minority families focussing on transitional points, strengths and acceptable support (Kemps, 1997).

Children are also not a homogenous group. The age ranges from childhood to adolescence incorporates several developmental stages which would suggest attention being paid to the design of developmentally appropriate methods of intervention. It is important in this context to continue the task of finding out what works best for which children in what circumstances, and to link this with why some children fail to develop mental health problems even in highly disadvantaged situations.

Children are sometimes thought of as empty vessels waiting to be filled up. They are considered by some to be miniature adults. Services for children and young people's mental health have consequently often been based on adult concepts, models, and practices. This has led to paternalistic, patronising practices that seek to emasculate children and stifle their creativity and wisdom. It is still a relatively radical idea to think that children and adolescents are different from adults in fundamental ways that require different ways of conceptualising their problems and providing appropriate services in response.

I believe that society is still at the beginning of a process of understanding childhood and adolescence in terms that are relevant to them, rather than to carers/parents or adult dominated institutions. That understanding can only come from more involvement from children and young people in research, in the design of the research, and in the process of the research. The job of adults is to facilitate and support them in gaining more control over their lives, and social workers are ideally placed to fulfil that role in empowering, participatory practice.

I hope this book succeeds in providing some resources and guidance to social workers who wish to develop their role in relation to the increasing demand for supportive intervention in the lives of troubled children, adolescents, and young people. I have tried to write the book and use material in a balanced user-friendly way in order to avoid as far as possible being too obscure or obtuse. I have also not refrained from being clear about where I feel there needs to be clarity in the direction practice should take. The reader should assess the material in terms of their own feelings, the evidence base, professional instincts and agency expectations and use what seems beneficial at the time but which can also be discarded at another time. I welcome comments and feedback on how the contents help or hinder practice.

The primary mental health practitioner is achieving a growing professional presence in CAMHS with many being recruited from among the ranks of qualified social workers. This book complements their training requirements as well as pre and post qualifying awards in the degree in social work. Practitioners will find it also contributes to the values, knowledge and skills requirements for the TOPPS workforce competencies and is consistent with the BASW code of ethics for social work. Above all I hope the book enables you to reflect on your practice and on your own history and how by combining both experiences, you can offer the most important resource to your clients-yourself.

Steven Walker
Autumn 2002

Useful resources and organisations

Advisory Centre for Education
1b Aberdeen Studios 22 Highbury Grove,
London, N5 2EA
Tel: 020 7354 8321

Asian Family Counselling Services
74 The Avenue,
London, W13 8LB
Tel: 020 8997 5749

Asylum Aid
244a Upper Street
London N1 1RU
Tel: 020 7359 4026
www.asylumaid.org.uk

Barnardo's
Tanners Lane
Barkingside
Ilford, IG6 1QG
Tel: 020 8550 8822
www.barnardos.ie

Black Information Link
The 1990 Trust
9 Cranmer Road
London SW9 6EJ
Tel: 020 7582 1990
www.blink.org.uk

Child Poverty Action Group
1–5 Bath Street
London EC1V 9PY
Tel: 020 7253 3406

Child Psychotherapy Trust
Star House 104 Grafton Road
London NW5 4BD
Tel: 020 7284 1355
www.cpt.co.uk

Childline
2nd Floor, Royal Mail Building
50 Studd Street
London N1 0QW
Tel: 020 7239 1000
www.childline.org.uk

Children's Legal Centre
University of Essex
Wivenhoe Park
Colchester CO4 3SQ
Tel: 01206 873820
www.essex.ac.uk/clc

Children's Rights Office
City Road
London EC1V 1LJ
Tel: 020 7278 8222
www.cro.org.uk

Children's Society
Edward Rudolf House
Margery Street
London WC1X 0JL
Tel: 020 7841 4436
www.the-childrens-society.org.uk

Commission for Racial Equality
Elliot House,
10–12 Allington Street
London SW1E 5EH
Tel: 020 7828 7022
www.cre.gov.uk

Coram Family
49 Mecklenburgh Square
London WC1N 2QA
Tel: 020 7520 0300
www.coram.org.uk

Disability Now
6 Market Road
London N7 9PW
Tel: 020 7619 7323
www.disabilitynow.org.uk

Drugscope
32–36 Longman Street
London SE1 0EE
Tel: 020 7928 1771
www.drugscope.org.uk

FOCUS
The Royal College of Psychiatrists
6th Floor 83 Victoria Street
London SW1H 0HW
Tel: 020 7227 0821
www.rcpsych.ac.uk/cru

Families Need Fathers
134 Curtain Road
London EC2A 3AR
Tel: 020 7613 5060
www.fnf.org.uk

Family Rights Group
Print House 18 Ashwin Street,
London E8 3DL
Tel: 020 7923 2628
www.frg.co.uk

Home Start
2 Salisbury Road
Leicester LE1 7QR
Tel: 011 6233 9955
www.home-start.org.uk

Institute of Family Therapy
24–32 Stephenson Way
London NW1 2HV
020 7391 9150
www.ift.org.uk

Kidscape
2 Grosvenor Gardens
London SW1W 9TR
Tel: 020 7730 3300
www.kidscape.org.uk

MIND
15–19 Broadway
London E15 4BQ
Tel: 020 8522 1728
www.mind.org.uk

Mental Health Foundation
20–21 Cornwall Terrace
London NW1 4QL
Tel: 020 7535 7400
www.mentalhealth.org.uk

NCH Action for Children
85 Highbury Park
London N5 1UD
Tel: 020 7704 7000
www.nchafc.org.uk

NSPCC
42 Curtain Road
London EC2A 3NH
Tel: 020 7825 2500
www.nspcc.org.uk

NAFSIYAT
278 Seven Sisters Road,
London, N4 2HY
Tel: 020 7263 4130

National Association of Young People's
Counselling and Advisory Services
17–23 Albion Road, Leicester, LE1 6GD
Tel: 01642 816846

National Autistic Society
393 City Road
London EC1V 1NE
Tel: 020 7833 2299

National Centre for Eating Disorders
54 New Road
Esher KT10 9NU
Tel: 01372 469493
www.eating-disorders.org.uk

National Children's Bureau
8 Wakley Street
London EC1V 7QE
Tel: 020 7843 6000
www.ncb.org.uk

National Family and Parenting Institute
520 Highgate Studios
53–79 Highgate Road
London NW5 1TL
Tel: 020 7424 3460
www.nfpi.org.uk

National Pyramid Trust
204 Church Road
London W7 3BP
Tel: 020 8579 5108

Parentline Plus
Unit 520 Highgate studios
53–79 Highgate Road
London NW5 1TL
Tel: 020 7209 2460
www.parentlineplus.org.uk

Race Equality Unit
Unit 27/28 Angel Gate, City Road
London EC1V 2PT
Tel: 020 7278 2331
www.reunet.demon.co.uk

Refugee Council
3–9 Bondway
London SW8 1SJ
Tel: 020 7820 3000

Save the Children
17 Grove Lane
London SE5 8RD
Tel: 020 7703 5400
www.savethechildren.org.uk

Stepfamilies UK
www.stepfamilies.co.uk

Tavistock Institute
120 Belsize Lane
London NW3 5BA
Tel: 0207 435 7111
www.tav-port.org.uk

Trust for the Study of Adolescence
23 New Road
Brighton BN1 1WZ
Tel: 01273 693311
www.tsa.uk.com

Values into Action
Oxford House, Derbyshire Street,
London, E2 6HG
Tel: 020 7729 5436

Voice for the Child in Care
Unit 4 Pride Court
80–82 White Lion Street,
London N1 9PF
Tel: 020 7833 5792

Who Cares Trust
152–160 City Road
London EC1V 2NP
Tel: 020 7251 3117
www.thewhocarestrust.org.uk

Women's Aid Federation
PO Box 391
Bristol BS99 7WS
Tel: 08457 023468

YMCA Dads and Lads Project
Dee Bridge House
25–27 Lower Bridge Street
Chester CH1 1RS
Tel: 01244 403090

Young Minds
102–108 Clerkenwell Road
London EC1M 5SA
Tel: 020 7336 8445
www.youngminds.org.uk

Youth Access
2 Taylors Yard 67 Alderbrook Road
London SW12 8AD
Tel: 020 8772 9900
www.yacess.co.uk

Youth in Mind
www.youthinmind.net

Bibliography

Ackroyd, J. and Pilkington, A. (1999) Childhood and the Construction of Ethnic Identities in a Global Age. *Childhood.* 6: 4, 443–54.

Adams, G., Gullotta, T. and Montemayor, R. (Eds.) (1992) *Adolescent Identity Formation*, New York, Sage.

Adams, R., Dominelli, L. and Payne, M. (1998) *Social Work: Themes, Issues and Critical Debates*. Basingstoke, Macmillan.

Adams, R., Dominelli, L. and Payne, M. (2002) *Critical Practice in Social Work*, Basingstoke, Palgrave.

Alderson, P. (1995) *Listening to Children. Children Ethics and Social Research.* London, Barnardo's.

Alderson, P. (2000) *Young Children's Rights*. London, Save the Children/Jessica Kingsley.

American Psychiatric Association. (1994) *Diagnostic and Statistical Manual of Mental Disorders, 4th edn. (DSM IV)*. Washington DC, American Psychiatric Association.

Amery, J., Tomkins, A. and Victor, C. (1995) The Prevalence of Behavioural Problems Amongst Homeless Primary School Children in an Outer London Borough: A Feasibility Survey. *Public Health.* 109: 421–4.

Anderson, K. and Anderson, L. (Eds.) (1995) *Mosby's Pocket Dictionary of Nursing, Medicine and Professions Allied to Medicine*. London, Mosby.

Appleby, L., Cooper, J. and Amos, T. (1999) Psychological Autopsy Study of Suicides by People Aged Under 35. *British Journal of Psychiatry.* 175: 168–74.

Arcelus, J., Bellerby, T. and Vostanis, V. (1999) A Mental Health Service For Young People in the Care of the Local Authority. *Clinical Child Psychology and Psychiatry*. 4: 2, 233–45.

Atkin, K. and Rollings, J. (1993) *Community Care in a Multi-Racial Britain: A Critical Review of the Literature*. London, HMSO.

Audit Commission. (1994) *Seen but not Heard.* London, HMSO.

Audit Commission. (1998) *Child and Adolescent Mental Health Services.* London, HMSO.

Audit Commission. (1999) *Children in Mind: Child and Adolescent Mental Health Services.* London, HMSO.

Audit Commission. (2000) *Another Country: Implementing Dispersal Under the Immigration and Asylum Act 1999*, London, HMSO.

Bagley, C. and Mallick, K. (1995) Negative Self Perception and Components of Stress in Canadian, British and Hong Kong Adolescents. *Perceptual Motor Skills*. 81: 123–7.

Bagley, C. and Mallick, K. (2000) How Adolescents Perceive Their Emotional Life, Behaviour, and Self-Esteem in Relation to Family Stressors: A Six-Culture Study. In Singh, N., Leung, J. and Singh, A. (2000) *International Perspectives on Child and Adolescent Mental Health.* Oxford, Elsevier.

Bagley, C. and Young, L. (1998) The Interactive Effects of Physical, Emotional, and Sexual Abuse on Adjustment in a Longtitudinal Cohort of 565 Children From Birth to Age 17. In Bagley, C. and Mallick, K (Eds.) *Child Sexual Abuse: New Theory and Research*. Aldershot, Ashgate.

Bailey, R. and Brake. (Eds.) (1980) *Radial Social Work and Practice,* London, Edward Arnold.

Baldwin, M. (2000) *Care Management and Community Care.* Aldershot, Ashgate.

Baradon, T., Sinason, V. and Yabsley, S. (1999) Assessment of Parents and Young Children: A Child Psychotherapy Point of View. *Child Care Health and Development.* 25: 1.

Barclay, P. (1982) *Social Workers Their Role and Tasks.* London: NISW/DHSS.

Barlow, J. (1998) Parent Training Programmes and Behaviour Problems: Findings From a Systematic Review. In Buchanan, A. and Hudson, B. (Eds.) *Parenting, Schooling, and Childrens Behaviour: Interdisciplinary Approaches.* Alton. Ashgate Publishers.

Barlow, J., McKie, L. and Grant-Richardson, P. (2001) *The Evaluation Journey: An Evaluation Pack for Community Groups.* Edinburgh: ASW Scotland.

Barnes, M., McGuire, J., Stein, A. and Rosenberg, W. (1997) Evidence Based Medicine and Child Mental Health Services. A Broad Approach to Evaluation is Needed. *Children and Society.* 11: 89–96.

Barnes, M. and Warren, L. (1999) *Paths to Empowerment.* Bristol, Policy Press.

Barry, M. and Hallett, C. (Eds.) (1998) *Social Exclusion and Social Work.* Lyme Regis, Russell House Publishing.

Barter, C. (1999) *Protecting Children From Racism and Racist Abuse: A Research Review.* London, NSPCC.

Barter, K. (2001) Building Community: A Conceptual Framework for Child Protection, *Child Abuse Review.* 10: 262–78.

Barton, J. (1999) Child and Adolescent Psychiatry. In Hill, M. (Ed.) *Effective Ways of Working With Children and Their Families.* London, Jessica Kingsley.

BASW. (2002) *The Code of Ethics for Social Work,* Birmingham, BASW.

Bateman, N. (2000) *Advocacy Skills for Health and Social Care Professionals.* London: Jessica Kingsley.

Bayley, R. (1998) *Transforming Children's Lives: The Importance of Early Intervention.* London, Family Policy Studies Centre.

Beckett, C. (2002) *Human Growth and Development.* London, Sage.

Beresford, B., Sloper, P., Baldwin, S. and Newman, T. (1996) *What Works in Services for Families With a Disabled Child?* Barkingside, Barnardo's.

Bernzweig, J., Takayama, J., Phibbs, C., Lewis, C. and Pantell, R. H. (1997) Gender Differences in Physician-Patient Communication. *Archives of Pediatric Adolescent Medicine.* 151: 586–91.

Bhugra, D. (1999) *Mental Health of Ethnic Minorities.* London, Gaskell.

Bhugra, D. and Bahl, V. (1999) *Ethnicity: an Agenda for Mental Health.* London, Gaskell.

Bhui, K. (1997) London's Ethnic Minorities and The Provision of Mental Health Services. In Johnson, et al. (Eds.) *London's Mental Health.* London, King's Fund Institute.

Bhui, K. and Olajide, D. (1999) *Mental Health Service Provision for A Multi-Cultural Society.* London, Saunders.

Bilton, T., Bonnet, K., Jones, P., Lawson, T., Skinner, D., Stanwick, M. and Webster, A. (2002) *Introductory Sociology.* 4th edn. Basingstoke: Palgrave Macmillan.

Blackwell, D. and Melzak, S. (2000) *Far From the Battle But Still at War: Troubled Refugee Children in School.* London, The Child Psychotherapy Trust.

Bochner, S. (1994) Cross-Cultural Differences in The Self-Concept: A Test of Hofstede's Individualism/Collectivism Distinction. *Journal of Cross-Cultural Psychology*. 2: 273–83.

Bourne, D. (1993) Over-Chastisement, Child Non-Compliance and Parenting Skills: A Behavioural Intervention by a Family Centre Social Worker. *British Journal of Social Work*. 5: 481–500.

Boyd-Franklin, N., Steiner, G. and Boland, M. (1995) *Children, Families and HIV/AIDS*, New York, Guilford Press.

Bradshaw, J. (Ed.) (2001) *Poverty: The Outcomes for Children*. London, Family Policy Studies Centre/ESRC.

Brammer, A. (2003) *Social Work Law*. Harlow, Pearson Education.

Brandon, M., Schofield, G. and Trinder, L. (1998) *Social Work With Children*. Basingstoke, Macmillan.

Braye, S. and Preston-Shoot, M. (1997) *Practising Social Work Law*, 2nd edn. London, Macmillan Palgrave.

Brearley, J. (1995) *Counselling and Social Work*. Buckingham, Open University Press.

Brown, B., Crawford, P. and Darongkamas, J. (2000) Blurred Roles and Permeable Boundaries: The Experience of Multidisciplinary Working in Community Mental Health. *Health and Social Care in The Community*. 8: 6, 425–35.

Burghes, L., Clarke, L. and Cronin, N. (1997) *Fathers and Fatherhood in Britain*, London, Family Policy Studies Centre.

Butrym, Z. (1976) *The Nature of Social Work*. London, Macmillan.

Caan, W. and Belleroche, J. (2002) *Drink, Drugs and Dependence*. London, Routledge.

Caesar, G., Parchment, M. and Berridge, D. (1994) *Black Perspectives on Services for Children in Need*. London, Barnardo's/NCB.

Calder, M., Peake, A. and Rose, K. (2001) *Mothers of Sexually Abused Children*. Lyme Regis, Russell House Publishing.

Canino, I. and Spurlock, J. (2000) 2nd edn., *Culturally Diverse Children and Adolescents: Assessment, Diagnosis and Treatment.* New York, Guilford Press.

Carr, A. (Ed.) (2000) *What Works for Children and Adolescents? A Critical Review of Psychological Interventions With Children, Adolescents and Their Families.* London, Routledge.

CCETSW. (1989) *Paper 30.Rules and Requirements for The Diploma in Social Work*. London, CCETSW.

Cederborg, A. (1997) Young Children's Participation in Family Therapy Talk. *The American Journal of Family Therapy*. 25: 28–38.

Chambers, R. (1997) *Whose Reality Counts? Putting The First Last*. London, Intermediate Technology.

Chand, A. (2000) The Over Representation of Black Children in The Child Protection System: Possible Causes,Consequences and Solutions. *Child and Family Social Work*. 5: 67–77.

Cheetham, J. (1997) The Research Perspective. In Davies, M. (Ed.) *The Blackwell Companion to Social Work*. Oxford. Blackwell.

Child Psycotherapy Trust (1998) *Is Child Psycotherapy Effective for Children and Young People?* London: CPT.

Children's Legal Centre. (1994) *Mental Health Handbook: A Guide to The Law Affecting Children and Young People*. London, The Children's Legal Centre.

Christiansen, E. and James, G. (Eds.) (2000) *Research With Children, Perspectives and Practices.* London, Falmer Press.

Clarke, L., Bradshaw, J. and Williams, J. (2001) *Family Diversity, Poverty and The Mental Well-Being of Young People.* London, Health Education Authority.

Cole, E., Leavey, G. and King, M. (1995) Pathways to Care for Patients With First Episode of Psychosis. A Comparison of Ethnic Groups. *British Journal of Psychiatry.* 167: 770–6.

Comte, A. (1852) *System of Positive Polity. Vol 2: Social Statistics. 3.* London, Longmans Green.

Cooper, P. (Ed.) (1999) *Understanding and Supporting Children With Emotional and Behavioural Difficulties.* London, Jessica Kingsley.

Copley, B. and Forryan, B. (1997) *Therapeutic Work With Children and Young People.* London, Cassell.

Corrigan, P. and Leonard, P. (1978) *Social Work Practice Under Capitalism: A Marxist Approach.* London, Macmillan.

Costner, R., Guttman, H., Sigal, J., Epstein, N. and Rakoff, V. (1971) Process and Outcome in Conjoint Family Therapy. *Family Process.* 10: 451–74.

Cote, G. L. (1997) Socio-Economic Attainment, Regional Disparities, and Internal Migration. *European Sociological Review.* 13: 1, 55–77.

Coulshed, V. and Orme, J. (1998) *Social Work Practice: an Introduction.* (3rd edn.) Basingstoke, Macmillan.

Courtney, M., Barth, R., Berrick, J., Brooks, D., Needell, B. and Park, L. (1996) Race and Child Welfare Services: Past Research and Future Directions. *Child Welfare.* LXXV: 2, Mar/Apr.

Cox, A. (1994) Diagnostic Appraisal. In Rutter et al. *Child and Adolescent Psychiatry.* London, Blackwell.

Crawford, M. and Kessel, A. (1999) Not Listening to Patients: The Use and Misuse of Patient Satisfaction Studies. *International Journal of Social Psychiatry.* 45: 1, 1–6.

Cross, T., Bazron, B., Dennis, K. and Isaacs, M. (1989) *Toward a Culturally Competent System of Care: A Monograph on Effective Services for Minority Children Who Are Severely Emotionally Disturbed.* Washington DC, Georgetown University Child Development Center.

Crutcher, R. (1943) Child Psychiatry: The History of Its Development. *Psychiatry.* 6: 191–201.

Currer, C. (2001) *Responding to Grief: Dying, Bereavement and Social Care.* Basingstoke, Palgrave.

Daines, R., Lyond, K. and Parsloe, P. (1990) *Aiming for Partnership.* Barkingside, Barnardo's.

Dallos, R. and Draper, R. (2000) An *Introduction to Family Therapy.* Buckingham, OU Press.

Davies, M. (1981) *The Essential Social Worker: A Guide to Positive Practice.* Aldershot, Arena.

Davies, M. (Ed.) (1997) *The Blackwell Companion to Social Work.* Oxford, Blackwell.

Davis, H. and Spurr, P. (1998) Parent Counselling: Evaluation of a Community Child Mental Health Service. *Journal of Child Psychology and Psychiatry.* 39: 365–76.

Davis, H., Spurr, P., Cox, A., Lynch, M., Von Roenne, A. and Hahn, K. (1997) A Description and Evaluation of a Community Child Mental Health Service. *Clinical Child Psychology and Psychiatry.* 2: 2, 221–38.

Davis, J., Rendell, P. and Sims, D. (1999) The Joint Practitioner: A New Concept in Professional Training. *Journal of Interprofessional Care*.13: 4, 395–404.

Debell, D. and Everett, G. (1997) *In a Class Apart: A Study of School Nursing*. Norwich. East Norfolk Health Authority.

Debell, D. and Walker, S. (2002) *Norfolk Family Support Teams Final Evaluation Report.* Chelmsford, APU Centre for Research in Health and Social Care.

Dennis, J. and Smith, T. (2002) Nationality, Immigration and Asylum Bill 2002: Its Impact on Children, *Childright*. 187: 16–7.

DfEE. (1998) Towards an Interdisciplinary Framework for Developing Work With Children and Young People. *Childhood Studies Discipline Network. Conference Presentation*: Cambridge, Robinson College.

Dimigen, G., Del Priore, C., Butler, S., Evans, S., Ferguson, L. and Swan, M. (1999) Psychiatric Disorder Among Children at Time of Entering Local Authority Care. *British Medical Journal*. 319: 675–6.

Dingwall, R. (1989) Some Problems About Predicting Child Abuse and Neglect. In Stevenson, O. (Ed.) *Child Abuse: Public Policy and Professional Practice*. Hemel Hempstead, Harvester Wheatsheaf.

Doel, M. and Marsh, P. (1992) *Task Centred Work*, Aldershot, Ashgate.

Dogra, N., Parkin, A., Gale, F. and Frake, C. (2002) *A Multidisciplinary Handbook of Child and Adolescent Mental Health for Front-Line Professionals.* London, Jessica Kingsley.

DoH. (1989) *The Children Act*. London, HMSO.

DoH. (1995) *A Handbook on Child and Adolescent Mental Health*. London, HMSO.

DoH. (1995) *Child Protection: Messages From Research.* London, HMSO.

DoH. (1998) *Modernising Mental Health Services: Safe, Supportive and Sensible*. London, HMSO.

DoH. (1999) *Working Together to Safeguard Children*. London, HMSO.

DoH. (1999) *LAC Circular. (99) 33. Quality Protects Programme: Transforming Children's Services 2000–01*. London, HMSO.

DoH. (1999) *The Health Act*. London, HMSO.

DoH. (2000) *Framework for the Assessment of Children in Need*. London, HMSO.

DoH. (2000) *National Service Framework for Mental Health*. London, HMSO.

DoH. (2000) Social Services Inspectorate: *Excellence Not Excuses: Inspection of Services for Ethnic Minority Children and Families*. London, HMSO.

DoH. (2001) *Children Looked After in England:2000/2001*, London, HMSO.

DoH. (2001) *Safeguarding Children in Whom Illness Is Induced or Fabricated by Carers With Parenting Responsibilities*. London, HMSO.

DoH and DfEE. (1996) *Children's Service Planning: Guidance for Inter-Agency Working*. London, HMSO.

DoH. (1999) *Innovations Fund. Specific Mental Health Grant*. London, HMSO.

DoH. (1997) *The New NHS: Modern, Dependable.* London, HMSO.

DoHSS (1985) *Social Work Decisions in Child Care.* London, HMSO.

Dominelli, L. (1988) *Anti-Racist Social Work.* Basingstoke, Macmillan.

Dominelli, L. (1996) Deprofessionalising Social Work: Equal Opportunities, Competences, and Postmodernism. *British Journal of Social Work*. 26: 2, 153–75.

Dominelli, L. (1998) Anti-Oppressive Practice in Context. In Adams R, Dominelli L. and

Payne, M. (Eds.) *Social Work: Themes, Issues and Critical Debates*. Basingstoke, Macmillan.

Dominelli, L. (1999) Neo-Liberalism, Social Exclusion and Welfare Clients in a Global Economy. *International Journal of Social Welfare*. 8: 1, 14–22.

Dominelli, L. (2002) Changing Agendas-Moving Beyond Fixed Identities in Anti-Oppressive Practice. In Tomlinson, D. and Trew, W. (Eds.) *Equalising Opportunities, Minimising Oppression*. London, Routledge.

Donnellan, C. (2000) *Self Harm and Suicide*. Cambridge, Independence.

Doyle, C. (1997) *Working With Abused Children*. Basingstoke, Macmillan/BASW.

Dulmus, C. and Rapp-Paglicci, L. (2000) The Prevention of Mental Disorders in Children and Adolescents: Future Research and Public-Policy Recommendations. *Families in Society: The Journal of Contemporary Human Services*. 81: 3, 294–303.

Dunn, S. (1999) *Creating Accepting Communities*. London. Mind Publications.

Durlak, J. and Wells, A. (1997) Primary Prevention Mental Health Programs for Children and Adolescents: A Meta-Analytic Review. *American Journal of Community Psychology*. 25: 2, 115–52.

Durlak, J. (1998) Primary Prevention Mental Health Programmes for Children and Adolescents are Effective. *Journal of Mental Health* 7: 5, 454–69

Eamon, M. K. (1994) Poverty and Placement Outcomes of Intensive Family Preservation Services. *Child and Adolescent Social Work Journal*. 11: 5, 349–61.

Early Childhood Education Forum. (1998) *Quality and Diversity in Early Learning*. London, National Children's Bureau.

Eayrs, C. and Jones, R. (1992) Methodological Issues and Future Directions in the Evaluation of Early Intervention Programmes. *Child, Care, Health and Development*. 18: 15–28.

Eber, L., Osuch, R. and Redditt, C. (1996) School-Based Applications of The Wraparound Process: Early Results on Service Provision and Student Outcomes. *Journal of Child and Family Studies*. 5: 83–99.

Eliason, M. (1996) Lesbian and Gay Family Issues. *Journal of Family Nursing*. 2: 1, 10–29.

Elliot, R. and Shapiro, D. (1992) Client and Therapists as Analysts of Significant Events. In Tonkmanianandd, S. G. (Ed.) *Psychotherapy Process Research, Paradigmatic Narrative Approaches*. Newbury Park. CA, Sage.

Ely, P. and Denney, P. (1987) *Social Work in A Multi-Racial Society*. London, Gower.

Erikson, E. (1965) *Childhood and Society*. Harmondsworth, Penguin.

Fagin, C. M. (1992) Collaboration Between Nurses and Physicians; No Longer A Choice. *Academic Medicine*. 67: 5, 295–303.

Falloon, I. and Fadden, G. (1995) *Integrated Mental Health Care: A Comprehensive Community-Based Approach*. Cambridge, Cambridge University Press.

Farrant, F. (2001) *Troubled Inside: Responding to The Mental Health Needs of Children and Young People in Prison*. London, Prison Reform Trust.

Farrington, D. (1995) The Development of Offending and Antisocial Behaviour From Childhood: Key Findings From The Cambridgeshire Study in Delinquent Development. *Journal of Child Psychology and Psychiatry*.

Fawcett, B. (2000) Look Listen and Learn. *Community Care*. July.

Fernando, S. (2002) *Mental Health Race and Culture*. Basingstoke, Palgrave.

Finch, J. (1987) The Vignette Technique in Survey Research. *Sociology.* 21: 1, 105–14.

Firth, M., Dyer, M. and Wilkes, J. (1999) Reducing The Distance: Mental Health Social Work in General Practice. *Journal of Interprofessional Care.* 13: 4, 335–44.

Fletcher-Campbell, F. (2001) Issues of Inclusion. *Emotional and Behavioural Difficulties.* 6: 2, 69–89.

Fombonne, E. (1995) Depressive Disorders: Time Trends and Possible Explanatory Mechanisms. In Rutter and Smith. *Psychosocial Disorders of Youth.* New York, Wiley.

Fook, J. (2002) *Social Work: Critical Theory and Practice.* London, Sage.

Fook, J., Ryan, M. and Hawkins, L. (1997) Towards a Theory of Social Work Expertise. *British Journal of Social Work.* 27: 399–417.

Franklin, A. and Madge, N. (2000) *In Our View: Children, Teenagers and Parents Talk About Services for Young People.* London, NCB.

Freeman, I., Morrison, A., Lockhart, F. and Swanson, M. (1996) Consulting Service Users:The Views of Young People. In Hill, M. and Aldgate, J. (Eds.) *Child Welfare Services: Developments in Law, Policy, Practice and Research.* London. Jessica Kingsley.

Freud, S. (1905) *Three Essays on The Theory of Sexuality. Standard Edition. Vol 6.* London, Hogarth Press.

Friedlander, M., Highlen, P. and Lassiter, W. (1985) Content Analytic Comparison of Four Expert Counsellors Appraoches to Family Treatment. *Journal of Counselling Psychology.* 32: 171–80.

Fuller, R. (1996) Evaluating Social Work Effectiveness: A Pragmatic Approach. In Alderson, et al. *What Works: Effective Social Interventions in Child Welfare.* Barkingside, Barnardo's.

Furlong, A. and Carmel, F. (1997) *Young People and Social Change.* Buckingham, Open University Press.

Gardner, R. (1998) *Family Support: A Practitioners Guide.* Birmingham, Venture Press.

Ghate, D. and Daniels, A. (1997) *Talking About My Generation.* London, NSPCC.

Ghate, D., Shaw, C. and Hazel, N. (2000) *Fathers and Family Centres.* York, Policy Research Bureau/JRF.

Gibbons, J. and Wilding, J. (1995) *Needs, Risks and Family Support Plans: Social Services Departments Responses to Neglected Children.* Norwich, University of East Anglia.

Gibson-Cline, J. (Ed.) (1996) *Adolescence: From Crisis to Coping.* London, Butterworth-Heinemann.

Giddings, F. H. (1898) *The Elements of Sociology.* New York, Macmillan.

Glaser, D., Prior, V. and Lynch, M. (2001) *Emotional Abuse and Emotional Neglect: Antecedents, Operational Definitions and Consequences.* York, BASPCAN/DoH.

Goodman, R. (1997) *Child and Adolescent Mental Health Services: Reasoned Advice to Commissioners and Providers. Discussion Paper No 4.* London, Maudsley Hospital.

Goodman, R. (1997) The Strengths and Difficulties Questionnaire: A Research Note. *Journal of Child Psychology and Psychiatry.* 38: 5, 581–6.

Goodman, R. and Scott, S. (1997) *Child Psychiatry.* London, Sage.

Gordon, G. and Grant, R. (1997) *How We Feel: an Insight Into the Emotional World of Teenagers.* London, Jessica Kingsley.

Gorell Barnes, G. (1998) *Family Therapy in Changing Times*, Basingstoke, Macmillan.

Gowers, S., Bailey-Rogers, S., Shore, A. and Levine, W. (2000) Health of The Nation Outcome Scales for Child and Adolescent Mental Health (HONOSCA). *Child Psychology and Psychiatry Review.* 5: 2, 50–6.

Gowers, S., Harrington, R., Whitton, A., Lelliot, P., Beevor, A., Wing, J. and Jezzard, R. (1999) Brief Scale for Measuring the Outcomes of Emotional and Behavioural Disorders in Children. *British Journal of Psychiatry.* 174: 413–6.

Graham, P. (1992) *Child Psychiatry: A Developmental Approach.* New York, Oxford University Press.

Graham, P. (1996) The Thirty Year Contribution of Research in Child Mental Health to Clinical Practice and Public Policy in The UK. In Bernstein, B. and Brannen, J. (Eds.) *Children Research and Policy.* London, Taylor and Francis.

Greenbaum, T. (1987) *The Practical Handbook and Guide to Focus Group Research.* Lexington, Lexington Books.

Grey, M. (1993) Stressors and Children's Health. *Journal of Pediatric Nursing.* 8: 2, 85–91.

Griffiths, R. (1998) *Educational Citizenship and Independent Learning.* London, Jessica Kingsley.

Gross, D., Fogg, L. and Tucker, S. (1995) The Efficacy of Parent Training for Promoting Positive Parent-Toddler Relationships. *Research in Nursing and Health.* 18: 489–99.

Gunnell, D., Wehner, H. and Frankel, S. (1999) Sex Differences in Suicide Trends in England and Wales. *The Lancet.* 353: 556–7.

Hacking, I. (1999) *The Social Construction of What?* London, Harvard University Press.

Hadfield, J. (1975) *Childhood and Adolescence.* London: Penguin.

Hague, G. and Malos, E. (1993) *Domestic Violence: Action for Change.* Cheltenham, New Clarion Press.

Hampson, S. (1995) The Construction of Personality. In Hampson, S. E. and Coleman, A. M. (Eds.) *Individual Differences and Personality.* London, Longman.

Hardiker, P. (1995) *The Social Policy Contexts of Services to Prevent Unstable Family Life.* York, Joseph Rowntree Foundation.

Hawton, K., Arensman, E. and Townsend, E. (1998) Deliberate Self Harm: Systematic Review of Efficacy of Psychosocial and Pharmacological Treatments in Preventing Repetition. *British Medical Journal.* 317: 441–7.

Hazel, N. (1995) *Seen and Heard: an Examination of Methods for Collecting Data From Young People.* Social Research Update. Guildford, University of Surrey.

Health Advisory Service (1995) *Together We Stand: Thematic Review on the Commissioning, Role and Management of CAMHS Services.* London: HMSO.

Healy, K. (2002) *Social Work Practices: Contemporary Perspectives on Change.* London, Sage.

Heath, I. (1994) The Poor Man at His Gate: Homelessness is an Avoidable Cause of Ill Health. *British Medical Journal.* 309: 1675–6.

Hellinckx, W., Colton, M. and Williams, M. (1997) *International Perspectives on Family Support.* Aldershot, Ashgate Publishing.

Hendrick, H. (1997) Constructions and Reconstructions of British Childhood: An Interpretive Survey 1800 to The Present. In James, A. and Prout, A. (Eds.) *Constructing and Reconstructing Childhood: Contemporary Issues of the Sociology of Childhood.* London, Falmer Press.

Hennessey, E. (1999) Children as Service Evaluators. *Child Psychology and Psychiatry Review.* 4: 4, 153–61.

Hester, M., Pearson, C. and Harwin, N. (2000) *Making an Impact: Children and Domestic Violence.* London, Jessica Kingsley.

Hetherington, R. and Baistow, K. (2001) Supporting Families With A Mentally Ill Parent: European Perspectives on Interagency Cooperation. *Child Abuse Review.* 10: 351–65.

Heyman, I., Fombonne, E., Simmons, H., Ford, T., Meltzer, H. and Goodman, R. (2001) Prevalence of Obsessive-Compulsive Disorder in The British Nationwide Survey of Child Mental Health. *British Journal of Psychiatry.* 179: 324–9.

Higgins, K., Pinkerton, J. and Devine, P. (1997) *Family Support in Northern Ireland: Pespectives From Practice.* Belfast, Centre for Child Care Research.

Hill, M., Laybourn, A. and Borland, M. (1996) Engaging With Primary-Age Children About Their Emotions and Well-Being: Methodological Considerations. *Children and Society.* 10: 129–44.

Hill, M. (1999) *Effective Ways of Working With Children and Their Families.* London, Jessica Kingsley.

HMSO. (1968) *Local Authority and Allied Personal Social Services. (Cm. 3703).* London, HMSO.

HMSO. (2000) *Social Inequalities in the United Kingdom.* London, Office for National Statistics.

Hodes, M. (1998) Refugee Children May Need A Lot of Psychiatric Help. *British Medical Journal.* 316: 793–4.

Hodes, M. (2000) Psychologically Distressed Refugee Children in The United Kingdom. *Child Psychology and Psychiatry Review.* 5: 2, 57–67.

Holt, C. (1998) Working With Fathers of Children in Need. In Bayley, R. (Ed.) *Transforming Childrens Lives: The Importance of Early Intervention.* London, Family Policy Studies Centre.

Holterman, S. (1995) *All Our Futures: The Impact of Public Expenditure and Fiscal Policies on Britain's Children and Young People.* Barkingside, Barnardo's.

Horwath, J. and Calder, M. (1998) Working Together to Protect Children on the Child Protection Register: Myth or Reality. *British Journal of Social Work.* 28: 879–95.

House of Commons. (1997) Child and Adolescent Mental Health Services. *Health Committee.* London, HMSO.

Howe, D. (1989) *The Consumers View of Family Therapy.* London, Gower.

Howe, D. (Ed.) (1999) *Attachment and Loss in Child and Family Social Work.* Aldershot, Ashgate.

Howe, D., Brandon, M., Hinings, D. and Schofield, G. (1999) *Attachment Theory, Child Maltreatment and Family Support.* Basingstoke, Macmillan.

Howe, G. (1999) *Mental Health Assessments.* London, Jessica Kingsley.

Hunter, J., Higginson, I. and Garralda, E. (1996) Systematic Literature Review: Outcome Measures for Child and Adolescent Mental Health Services. *Journal of Public Health Medicine.* 18: 197–206.

Hutchings, J., Nash, S., Smith, M. and Parry, G. (1998) *Long-Term Outcome for Pre-School Children Referred to CAMH Team for Behaviour Management Problems.* Bangor, School of Psychology, University of Wales.

Imam, U. (1994) Asian Children and Domestic Violence. In Mullender, A. and Morley, R. (Eds.) *Children Living With Domestic Violence.* London, Whiting and Birch.

Iwaniec, D. (1995) *The Emotionally Abused and Neglected Child: Identification, Assessment and Intervention.* Chichester, Wiley.

James, A. and Prout, A. (Eds.) (1990) *Constructing and Reconstructing Childhood.* Basingstoke, Falmer.

JCWI. (2002) *Joint Council for The Welfare of Immigrants Response to The White Paper Secure Borders, Safe Haven: Integration With Diversity in Modern Britain.* London, JCWI.

Jenks, C. (1996) *Childhood.* London, Routledge.

Jones, C. (1997) Poverty. In Davies, M. (Ed.) *The Blackwell Companion to Social Work.* Oxford, Blackwell.

Jones, D. and Jones, M. (1999) The Assessment of Children With Emotional and Behavioural Difficulties: Psychometrics and Beyond. In Cooper, C. (Ed.) *Understanding and Supporting Children With Emotional and Behavioural Difficulties.* London, Jessica Kingsley.

Jordan, B. (1990) *Social Work in an Unjust Society.* Hemel Hempstead, Harvester Wheatsheaf.

Kalnins, I., Mcqueen, D., Backett, K., Curtice, L. and Currie, C. (1992) Children Empowerment and Health Promotion: Some New Directions in Research and Practice. *Health Promotion International.* 7: 1, 53–9.

Kashani, J. and Allan, W. (1998) *The Impact of Family Violence on Children and Adolescents.* London, Sage.

Kay-Shuttleworth, J. (1832) *The Moral and Physical Condition of The Working Classes Employed in the Cotton Manufacture in Manchester.* Ridgway (1987) Reprint Burney, E. L., Liverpool, Acorn Press.

Kelson, M. (1997) *Consumer Involvement Initiatives in Clinical Audit and Outcomes.* London, College of Health.

Kemps, C. (1997) Approaches to Working With Ethnicity and Cultural Issues. In Dwivedi, K. (Ed.) *Enhancing Parenting Skills.* London, Wiley.

Kemshall, H. (1993) Assessing Competence: Process or Subjective Inference? Do We Really See It? *Social Work Education.* 12: 1, 36–45.

Kent, H. and Read, J. (1998) Measuring Consumer Participation in Mental Health Services: Are Attitudes Related to Professional Orientation? *International Journal of Social Psychiatry.* 44: 4, 295–310.

Kiddle, C. (1999) *Traveller Children: A Voice for Themselves.* London, Jessica Kingsley.

Kim, W. J. (1995) A Training Guideline of Cultural Competence for Child and Adolescent Psychiatric Residencies. *Child Psychiatry and Human Development.* 26: 2, 125–36.

Kitzinger, J. (1994) The Methodology of Focus Groups: The Importance of Interaction Between Research Participants. *Sociology of Health and Fitness.* 16: 1, 103–20.

Knapp, M. and Scott, S. (1998) *Lifetime Costs of Conduct Disorder.* London: MIND.

Kolbo, J., Blakley, E. and Engelman, D. (1996) Children Who Witness Domestic Violence: A Review of Empirical Literature. *Journal of Interpersonal Violence.* 11: 2, 281–93.

Kraemer, S. (1995) What Are Fathers For? In Burcke, C. and Speed, B. (Eds.) *Gender, Power and Relationships.* London, Routledge.

Kurtz, Z. (1992) (Ed.) *With Health in Mind Quality Review Series on Mental Health Care for*

Children and Young People. London, Action for Sick Children/SW Thames Regional Health Authority.

Kurtz, Z. (1996) *Treating Children Well: A Guide to Using the Evidence Base in Commissioning and Managing Services for The Mental Health of Children and Young People.* London, Mental Health Foundation.

Kurtz, Z. (2001) *Report on Evaluation of CAMHS Innovation Projects.* London, Young Minds.

Kurtz, Z., Thornes, R. and Wolkind, S. (1994) *Services for the Mental Health of Children and Young People in England: A National Review.* London, SW Thames Regional Health Authority and DoH.

Kurtz, Z., Thornes, R. and Wolkind, S. (1995) *Services for the Mental Health of Children and Young People in England: Assessment of Needs and Unmet Need.* London, HMSO.

Lader, D., Singleton, N. and Meltzer, H. (1997) *Psychiatric Morbidity Among Young Offenders in England and Wales.* London, HMSO.

Laing, R. D. (1969) Interventions in Social Situations. Philadelphia Association. Cited in *Context.* 60: 2–7, Apr. Warrington Association for Family Therapy and Systemic Practice.

Lane, M. (1997) Community Work, Social Work: Green and Postmodern? *British Journal of Social Work.* 27: 319–41.

Lansdowne, G. (1995) *Taking Part: Children's Participation in Decision-Making.* London, IPPR.

Lask, J. and Lask, B. (1981) *Child Psychiatry and Social Work.* London, Tavistock.

Laws, S., Armitt, D., Metzendorf, W., Percival, P. and Reisel, J. (1999) *Time to Listen: Young People's Experiences of Mental Health Services.* London, Save The Children.

Leathard, A. (1994) *Going Inter-Professional.* London, Routledge.

Leonard, P. (1994) Knowledge/Power and Postmodernism: Implications for The Practice of a Critical Social Work Education. *Canadian Social Work Review.* 11: 1, 11–26.

Leonard, P. (1997) *Postmodern Welfare: Reconstructing an Emancipatory Project.* London, Sage.

Levine, H. (1993) Context and Scaffolding in Developmental Studies of Mother-Child Problem-Solving Dyads. In Chaiklin, S. and Lave, J. (Eds.) *Understanding Practice.* Cambridge, Cambridge University Press.

Little, M and Mount, K. (1999) *Prevention and Early Intervention With Children in Need.* Aldershot, Ashgate.

Llewelyn, S. (1988) Psychological Therapy as Viewed by Clients and Therapists. *British Journal of Clinical Psychology.* 27: 223–37.

Lloyd, E. (1999) (Ed.) *Parenting Matters: What Works in Parenting Education?* London, Barnardo's.

Lyon, J., Dennison, C. and Wilson, A. (2000) *Tell Them So they Listen. Messages From Young People in Custody. Home Office Research Study 201,* London, HMSO.

Lyons, P., Doueck, H. and Wodarski, J. (1996) Risk Assessment for Child Protective Services: A Review of the Empirical Literature on Instrument Performance. *Social Work Research.* 20: 3, 143–55.

Macdonald, G. (1999) Social Work and Its Evaluation: A Methodological Dilemma? In Williams, F., Popay, J. and Oakley, A. *Welfare Research: A Critical Review.* London, UCL Press.

Macdonald, G. and Roberts, H. (1995) *What Works in The Early Years? Effective Interventions for Children and Their Families.* Barkingside, Barnardo's.

MacFarlane, A. and McPherson, A. (1995) Primary Healthcare and Adolescence. *British Medical Journal.* 311: 825–6.

Madge, N. (2001) *Understanding Difference: The Meaning of Ethnicity for Young Lives.* London, National Children's Bureau.

Magrab, P., Evans, P. and Hurrell, P. (1997) Integrated Services for Children and Youth at Risk: an International Study of Multidisciplinary Training. *Journal of Interprofessional Care.* 11: 1, 99–108.

Malek, M. (1993) *Passing The Buck: Institutional Responses to Children With Difficult Behaviour.* London, Children's Society.

Marsh, P. (1997) Task-Centred Work. In Davies, M. (Ed.) *The Blackwell Companion to Social Work.* Oxford, Blackwell.

Marshal, M., Feldman, R. and Sigal, J. (1989) The Unravelling of a Treatment Paradigm: A Follow-Up Study of The Milan Approach to Family Therapy. *Family Process.* 28: 457–70.

Martin, G., Rozanes, P., Pearce, C. and Alison, S. (1995) Adolescent Suicide, Depression and Family Dysfunction. *Acta Psychiatrica Scandinavica.* 92: 336–44.

Mas, C., Alexander, J. and Barton, C. (1985) Modes of Expression in Family Therapy: A Process Study of Roles and Gender. *Journal of Family and Marital Therapy.* 11: 411–5.

May, T. (Ed.) (2002) *Qualitative Research in Action.* London, Sage.

Mayall, B. (1994) *Children's Childhood Observed and Experienced.* Lewes, Falmer Press.

McCabe, M. and Ricciardelli, L. (2001) Body Image and Body Change Techniques Among Young Adolescent Boys. *European Eating Disorders Review.* 9: 335–47.

McCann, J., James, A., Wilson, S. and Dunn, G. (1996) Prevalence of Psychiatric Disorders in Young People in the Care System. *British Medical Journal.* 313: 1529–30.

McClelland, M. and Sands, R. (2002) *Interprofessional and Family Discourses.* New Jersey, Hampton Press.

McClure, G. (2001) Suicide in Children and Adolescents in England and Wales 1970–1998. *British Journal of Psychiatry.* 178: 469–74.

McConville, B. (2001) *Saving Young Lives: Calls to Childline About Suicide.* London, Childline.

McGlone, F., Park, A. and Smith, K. (1998) *Families and Kinship.* London, Family Policy Studies Centre.

McGuire, J. B., Stein, A. and Rosenberry, W. (1997) Evidence-Based Medicine and Child Mental Health Services. *Children and Society.* 11: 2, 89–96.

McGurk, H. (Ed.) (1992) *Childhood and Social Development.* London, Lawrence Earlbaum.

Meltzer, H., Gatward, R., Goodman, R. and Ford, T. (2000) *Mental Health of Children and Adolescents in Great Britain.* London, HMSO.

Mental Health Foundation. (1993) *Mental Illness: The Fundamental Facts.* London, Mental Health Foundation.

Mental Health Foundation. (1999) *The Big Picture: Promoting Children and Young People's Mental Health.* London, Mental Health Foundation.

Mental Health Foundation. (2001) *Turned Upside Down.* London, Mental Health Foundation.

Mental Health Foundation. (2002) *The Mental Health Needs of Young Offenders.* London, Mental Health Foundation.

Micklewright, J. and Stewart, K. (2000) Well Being of Children in The European Union. *New Economy.* London, Institute for Public Policy Research.

Middleton, L. (1997) *The Art of Assessment.* Birmingham, Venture Press.

Midgley, J. (2001) Issues in International Social Work: Resolving Critical Debates in The Profession. *Journal of Social Work.* 1: 1, 21–35.

Miller, G. and Prinz, R. (1990) Enhancement of Social Learning Family Interventions for Childhood Conduct Disorders. *Psychological Bulletin.* 108: 291–307.

Mills, R. and Duck, S. (2000) *The Developmental Psychology of Personal Relationships.* Chichester, Wiley.

Milner, J. and O'Byrne, P. (1998) *Assessment in Social Work Practice.* London, Macmillan.

Mishra, R. (1999) *Globalization and the Welfare State.* Northampton MA, Edward Elgar.

Modood, T. and Berthoud, R. (1997) *Ethnic Minorities in Britain.* London, Policy Studies Institute.

Moffic, H. and Kinzie, J. (1996) The History and Future of Cross-Cultural Psychiatric Services. *Community Mental Health Journal.* 32: 6, 581–92.

Morris, J. (1998) *Accessing Human Rights: Disabled Children and The Children Act.* Barkingside, Barnardo's.

Morris, K. and Tunnard, J. (1996) *Family Group Conferences: Messages From UK Practice and Research.* London, Family Rights Group.

Morrison, L. and L'Heureux, J. (2001) Suicide and Gay/Lesbian/Bisexual Youth: Implications for Clinicians. *Journal of Adolescence.* 24: 39–49.

Morrissey, J., Johnsen, M. and Calloway, M. (1997) Evaluating Performance and Change in Mental Health Systems Serving Children and Youth: An Inter-organizational Network Approach. *The Journal of Mental Health Administration.* 24: 1, 4–22.

Morrow, V. (1998) *Understanding Families: Children's Perspectives.* London, National Children's Bureau.

Morrow, V. and Richards, M. (1996) The Ethics of Social Research With Children: an Overview. *Children and Society.* 10: 90–105.

Mullender, A and Ward, D. (1991) *Self-directed Groupwork: Users Take Action for Empowerment.* London: Whiting & Birch.

Mullender, A., Burton, S., Hague, G., Malos, E. and Imam, U. (2000) *Children's Needs, Coping Strategies and Understanding of Woman Abuse.* Coventry, Warwick University.

Mun, E., Fitzgerald, H., Von Eye, A., Puttler, L. and Zucker, R. (2001) Temperamental Characteristics as Predictors of Externalising and Internalising Child Behaviour Problems in The Contexts of High and Low Parental Psychpathology. *Infant Mental Health Journal.* 22: 3, 393–415.

Munley, A., Powers, C. S. and Williamson, J. B. (1982) Humanising Nursing Home Environments: The Relevance of Hospice Principles. *International Journal of Ageing and Human Development.* 15: 263–84.

Murdock, G. (1949) *Social Structure.* New York, Macmillan.

Nathanson, V. (2001) Health and Children's Rights: Inequality, Autonomy and Consent to Treatment. Childright. 161: 11–3.

NCH Action for Children. (2000) *Fact File.* London, NCH.

Newbigging, K. (2001) Promoting Social Inclusion. *The Mental Health Review.* 6: 3, 5–12.

NHS Health Advisory Service. (1995) *Together We Stand: Child and Adolescent Mental Health Services.* London, HMSO.

NISW. (1982) *Social Workers: Their Role and Tasks*. London, NISW/Bedford Square Press.

Nixon, C. and Northrup, D. (1997) Evaluating Mental Health Services: How Do Programs for Children Work in The Real World? Thousand Oaks, Sage.

O'Connor, P. and Neugebauer, R. (1992) The Contribution of Maternal Depressive Symptoms and Life Events to Child Behaviour Problems. *Paediatric and Perinatal Epidemiology*. 6: 254–64.

O'Donnell, G. (2002) *Mastering Sociology*. London, Palgrave.

O'Hagan, K. (Ed.) (1996) *Competence in Social Work Practice*. London, Jessica Kingsley.

O'Sullivan, T. (1999) *Decision Making in Social Work*. London, Macmillan.

Oberhuemer, P. (1998) A European Perspective on Early Years Training. In Abbott, L. and Pugh, G. (Eds.) *Training to Work in the Early Years: Developing the Climbing Frame*. Buckingham, OUP.

Oberklaid, F., Sanson, A., Pedlow, R. and Prior, M. (1993) Predicting Pre School Behaviour Problems From Temperament and Other Variables in Infancy. *Pediatrics*. 91: 1, 113–20.

Office for National Statistics. (2001) *Child and Adolescent Mental Health Statistics*. London, HMSO.

Office for National Statistics. (2002) *Social Tends 32*. London, HMSO.

OFSTED. (1996) *Exclusions From Secondary Schools 1995–96*. London, HMSO.

Onyet, S., Heppleston, T. and Bushnell, N. (1994) *A National Survey of Community Mental Health Teams: Team Structure*. London, Sainsbury Centre for Mental Health.

Oosterhorn, R. and Kendrick, A. (2001) No Sign of Harm: Issues for Disabled Children Communicating About Abuse. *Child Abuse Review*. 10: 243–53.

Oullette, P., Lazear, K. and Chambers, K. (1999) Action Leadership: The Development of an Approach to Leadership Enhancement for Grassroots Community Leaders in Children's Mental Health. *The Journal of Behavioural Health Services and Research*. 26: 2, 171–85.

Ovretveit, J. (1996) Five Ways to Describe A Multidisciplinary Team. *Journal of Interprofessional Care*. 10: 2, 163–71.

Owen, D. (1992–1995) *1991 Census Statistical Papers 1–9, Centre for Research in Ethnic Relations*. London, University of Warwick/Commission for Racial Equality.

Parsloe, P. (1999) (Ed.) *Risk Assessment in Social Care and Social Work*. London, Jessica Kingsley.

Parton, N. (1994) The Nature of Social Work Under Conditions of (Post) Modernity. *Social Work and Social Sciences Review*. 5: 2, 93–112.

Parton, N. (1999) Reconfiguring Child Welfare Practices: Risk, Advanced Liberalism and The Government of Freedom. In Chambon, A. S., Irving, A. and Epstein, L. (Eds.) *Reading Foucault for Social Work*. Chichester, Columbia Press.

Parton, N. and O'Byrne, P. (2001) *Constructive Social Work*. Basingstoke, Palgrave.

Payne, M. (1997) *Modern Social Work Theory*. London, Macmillan.

Pearce, J. (1999) Collaboration Between the NHS and Social Services in The Provision of Child and Adolescent Mental Health Services: A Personal View. *Child Psychology and Psychiatry Review*. 4: 4, 150–3.

Pease, B. and Fook, J. (Eds.) (1999) *Transforming Social Work Practice: The Challenge of Postmodernism*. London, Routledge.

Pentini-Aluffi, A. and Lorenz, W. (1996) *Anti Racist Work With Young People*. Lyme Regis, Russell House Publishing.

Piaget, J. (1953) *The Origin of Intelligence in The Child*. London, Routledge, Kegan Paul.

Pickering, W. (1979) *Durkheim: Essays on Morals and Education*. London, Routledge.

Pickles, A., Rowe, R., Simonoff, E., Foley, D., Rutter, M. and Silberg, J. (2001) Child Psychiatric Symptoms and Psychosocial Impairment: Relationship and Prognostic Significance. *British Journal of Psychiatry*. 179: 230–5.

Pierson, J. (2002) *Tackling Social Exclusion*. London, Routledge.

Pincus, A. and Minahan, A. (1973) Social Work Practice: Model and Method. Ithaca, IL, Peacock.

Pinkerton, J., Higgins, K. and Devine, P. (2000) *Family Support: Linking Project Evaluation to Policy Analysis*. Aldershot, Ashgate.

Pollard, A. (1987) Studying Childrens Perspectives: A Collaborative Approach. In Walford, G. (Ed.) *Doing Sociology of Education*. Lewes, Falmer Press.

Pollock, S. and Boland, M. (1990) Children and HIV Infection. *New Jersey Psychologist*. 40: 3, 17–21.

Polowczyk, D. (1993) Comparison of Patient and Staff Surveys of Consumer Satisfaction. *Hospital and Community Psychiatry*. 14: 4, 88–95.

Powell, F. (2001) *The Politics of Social Work*. London, Sage.

Powell, J. and Lovelock, R. (1992) *Changing Patterns of Mental Health Care*. London, Avebury.

Pringle, N. and Thompson, P. (1999) *Social Work, Psychiatry and The Law*. Aldershot, Ashgate.

Pugh, G. and Smith, C. (1996) *Learning to Be A Parent*. London, Family Policy Studies Centre.

Qureshi, T., Berridge, D. and Wenman, H. (2000) *Where to Turn? Family Support for South Asian Communities: A Case Study*. London, National Children's Bureau/JRF.

Ramon, S. (1999) Social Work. In Bhui K and Olajide D (Eds). *Mental Health Service Provision for a Multi-Cultural Society*. London, Saunders.

Ranger, T., Samad, S. and Stuart, O. (Eds.) (1996) *Culture Identity and Politics*. Aldershot, Avebury.

Rawson, D. (1994) Models of Interprofessional Work: Likely Theories and Possibilities. In Leathard, A. (Ed.) *Going Interprofessional: Working Together for Health and Welfare*. London, Routledge.

Read, J. and Barker, S. (1996) *Not Just Sticks and Stones. A Survey of the Stigma, Taboo and Discrimination Experienced by People With Mental Health Problems*. London, MIND.

Remschmidt, H. (2001) (Ed.) *Schizophrenia in Children and Adolescents*. Cambridge, Cambridge University Press.

Repper, J., Sayce, L., Strong, S., Wilmot, J. and Haines, M. (1997) *Tall Stories From The Back Yard*. London, MIND.

Richardson, J. and Joughin, C. (2000) *The Mental Health Needs of Looked After Children*. London, Gaskell.

Richmond, M. (1922) *What Is Social Casework?* New York, Russell Sage.

Robbins, D. (1998) The Refocusing Children's Initiative: an Overview of Practice. In Bayley, R. (Ed.) *Transforming Children's Lives: The Importance of Early Intervention*. London, Family Policy Studies Centre.

Robinson, L. (2001) A Conceptual Framework for Social Work Practice With Black Children and Adolescents in The United Kingdom. *Journal of Social Work*. 1: 2, 165–85.

Robinson, L. (1995) *Psychology for Social Workers: Black Perspectives*. London, Routledge.

Rodney, C. (2000) Pathways: A Model Service Delivery System. In Singh, N. N., Leung, J. P. and Singh, A. N. *International Perspectives on Child and Adolescent Mental Health*. London, Elsevier.

Rogers, C. (1951) *Client-Centred Therapy*. Boston, MA, Houghton Mifflin.

Rogers, C. (1957) The Necessary and Sufficient Conditions of Therapeutic Personality Change, *Journal of Consulting Psychology*, 21: 95–103.

Rogers, C. (1975) Empathic: an Unappreciated Way of Being. *Counselling Psychologis.*, 5: 2–10.

Rossi, P. H. (1992) Assessing Family Preservation Programmes. *Children and Youth Services Review*. 14: 77–97.

Roth, A. and Fonagy, P. (1996) *What Works for Whom? A Critical Review of Psychotherapy Research*. London, Guilford Press.

Royal College of Psychiatrists. (2002) *Parent-Training Programmes for the Management of Young Children With Conduct Disorders, Findings From Research*. London, RCP.

Russell, M. (1990) *Clinical Social Work: Research and Practice*. Newbury Park, Sage.

Rutter, M. (1985) Resiliance in The Face of Adversity. *British Journal of Psychiatry*. 147: 598–611.

Rutter, M. (1991) Services for Children With Emotional Disorders. *Young Minds Newsletter*. 9: 1–5.

Rutter, M. (1999) Preventing Anti-Social Behaviour in Young People: The Contribution of Early Intervention. In Bayley, R. (Ed.) *Transforming Children's Lives: The Importance of Early Intervention*. London, Family Policy Studies Centre.

Rutter, M. (Ed) (1995) *Psychosocial Disturbances in Young People: Challenges for Prevention*. Cambridge. Cambridge University Press.

Rutter, M. and Smith, D. (1995) *Psychosocial Disorders in Young People*. London, Wiley.

Rutter, M., Hersov, L. and Taylor, E. (1994) *Child and Adolescent Psychiatry*. Oxford, Blackwell Scientific.

Ryan, M. (1999) *The Children Act 1989: Putting It Into Practice*. Aldershot, Ashgate.

Saint-Exupery, A. (1943) *The Little Prince*. London, Heinemann.

Salmon, D. and Hall, C. (1999) Working With Lesbian Mothers: Their Healthcare Experiences. *Community Practitioner*. 72: 12, 396–7.

Salzberger-Wittenberg, I. (1981) *Psycho-Analytic Insight and Relationships*. London, Routledge.

Sandbaek, M. (1999) Children with Problems: Focusing on Everyday Life. *Children and Society*. 13: 106–18.

Sanford, M., Offord, D., Boyle, M., Pearce, A. and Racine, Y. (1992) Ontario Child Health Study: Social and School Impairments in Children Aged 6–16 Years. *Journal of The American Academy of Child and Adolescent Psychiatry*. 31: 1, 66–75.

Save The Children. (2001) *Denied a Future? The Right to Education of Roma/Gypsy Traveller Children in Europe*. London, Save The Children.

Save The Children Fund. (1995) *Towards A Children's Agenda*. London, Save The Children.

Savin-Williams, R. (2001) A Critique of Research on Sexual Minority Youth, *Journal of Adolescence*, 24: 5–13.

Sayce, L. and Measey, I. (1999) Strategies to Reduce Social Exclusion for People With Mental Health Problems. *Psychiatric Bulletin.* 23: 65–7.

Sebuliba, D. and Vostanis, P. (2001) Child and Adolescent Mental Health Training for Primary Care Staff. *Clinical Child Psychology and Psychiatry.* 6: 2, 191–204.

Shah, R. (1992) *The Silent Minority: Children With Disabilities in Asian Families.* London, National Children's Bureau.

Shah, R. (1994) Practice With Attitude: Questions on Cultural Awareness Training. *Child Health.* Apr/May.

Shapiro, J., Welker, C. and Jacobson, B. (1997) The Youth Client Satisfaction Questionnaire: Development, Construct, Validation, and Factor Structure. *Journal of Child Clinical Psychology.* 26: 87–98.

Shardlow, S. and Payne, M. (1998) *Contemporary Issues in Social Work: Western Europe.* Aldershot, Arena.

Sharman, W. (1997) *Children and Adolescents With Mental Health Problems.* London, Bailliere Tindall.

Shaw, I. (1996) *Evaluating in Practice.* Aldershot, Arena.

Shaw, I. (1999) *Qualitative Evaluation.* London, Sage.

Sheldon, B. and Chilvers, R. (2000) *Evidence-Based Social Care.* Lyme Regis, Russell House Publishing.

Simonian, S. J., Tarowski, K., Park, A. and Bekney, P. (1993) Child, Parent, and Physician Perceived Satisfaction With Pediatric Outpatient Visits. *Developmental and Behavioral Pediatrics.* 14: 8–12.

Sinclair, R., Garnett, L. and Berridge, D. (1995) *Social Work and Assessment With Adolescents.* London, National Children's Bureau.

Singh, N., Leung, J. and Singh, A. (2000) *International Perspectives on Chld and Adolescent Mental Health.* Oxford, Elsevier.

Skerrett, D. (2000) Social Work: A Shifting Paradigm. *Journal of Social Work Practice.* 14: 1, 63–73.

Skinner, B. (1953) *Science and Human Behaviour.* New York, Macmillan.

Smaje, C. (1995) *Health, Race and Ethnicity: Making Sense of The Evidence.* London, Kings Fund Institute.

Smale, G., Tuson, G. and Statham, D. (2000) *Social Work and Social Problems.* Basingstoke, Palgrave.

Smith, D., Mcara, L. and Mcvie, S. (2001) *The Edinburgh Study of Youth Transitions.* Edinburgh, Edinburgh University.

Smith, S., Rosen, K., Mccollum, E., Coleman, J. and Herman, S. (1996) The Voices of Children: Pre Adolescent Childrens Experiences in Family Therapy. *Journal of Marital and Family Therapy.* 22: 69–86.

Snelgrove, S. and Hughes, D. (2000) Interprofessional Relations Between Doctors and Nurses: Perspectives From South Wales. *Journal of Advanced Nursing.* 31: 3, 661–7.

Social Exclusion Unit. (2002) *Reducing Re-Offending by Ex-Offenders.* London, HMSO.

Social Services Inspectorate. (2000) *Excellence Not Excuses: Inspection of Services for Ethnic Minority Children and Families.* London, HMSO.

Social Services Inspectorate. (1998) *Partners in Planning: Approaches to Planning Services for Children and Their Families.* London. HMSO.

Solomos, J. (1989) *Race and Racism in Contemporary Britain.* Basingstoke, Macmillan.

Speak, S., Cameron, S., Woods, R. and Gilroy, R. (1995) *Young Single Mothers: Barriers to Independent Living.* London, Family Policy Studies Centre.

Stahmann, R. (2000) Premarital Counselling: A Focus for Family Therapy. *Journal of Family Therapy.* 22: 104–16.

Stanley, K. (2001) *Cold Comfort: Young Separated Refugees in England.* London, Save The Children.

Stanton, M. and Shadish, W. (1997) Outcome, Attrition and Family-Couples Treatment for Drug Abuse: A Meta-Analysis and Review of The Controlled Comparative Studies. *Psychological Bulletin.* 122: 170–91.

Statham, J. (2000) *Outomes and Effectiveness of Family Support Services: A Research Review.* London, Institute for Education, University of London.

Stephens, J. (2002) *The Mental Health Needs of Homeless Young People.* London, Mental Health Foundation.

Stephens, S. (Ed.) (1995) *Children and The Politics of Culture.* Princeton NJ, Princeton University Press.

Stepney, R. and Ford, S. (2000) *Social Work Models, Methods, and Theories.* Lyme Regis, Russell House.

Strickland Clark, L., Campbell, D. and Dallos, R. (2000) Children's and Adolescent's Views on Family Therapy. *Journal of Family Therapy.* 22: 324–41.

Stuntzer-Gibson, D., Koren, P. and Dechillo, N. (1995) The Youth Satisfaction Questionnaire: What Kids Think of Services. *Families in Society.* 76: 616–24.

Sutton, C. (1999) *Helping Families With Troubled Children.* London, Wiley.

Sutton, C. (2000) *Child and Adolescent Behaviour Problems.* Leicester, BPS.

Sylva, K. (1994) School Influences on Children's Development. *Journal of Child Psychology and Psychiatry.* 35: 1, 135–70.

Target, M. and Fonagy, P. (1996) The Psychological Treatment of Child and Adolescent Psychiatric Disorders. In Rothand, A. and Fonagy, P. (Eds.) *What Works for Whom? A Critical Review of Psychotherapy Research.* New York. The Guilford Press.

Taylor, B. and Devine, D. (1993) *Assessing Needs and Planning Care in Social Work.* London, Arena.

Taylor, C. and White, S. (2000) *Practising Reflexivity in Health and Welfare.* Buckingham, Open University Press.

Thoburn, J., Wilding, J. and Watson, J. (1998) *Children in Need: A Review of Family Support Work in Three Local Authorities.* Norwich. University of East Anglia/DoH.

Thomas, N. and O'Kane, C. (1998) The Ethics of Participatory Research With Children. *Children and Society.* 12: 82–96.

Thompson, N. (1995) *Theory and Practice in Health and Social Welfare.* Buckingham, Open University Press.

Thompson, N. (2001) *Anti-Discriminatory Practice.* London, Palgrave.

Thompson, N. (2001) *Understanding Social Work.* Basingstoke, Palgrave.

Thompson, N. (2002) *Building The Future: Social Work With Children, Young People and Their Families.* Lyme Regis, Russell House Publishing.

Tiller, P. (1988) Barn Som Sakkyndige Informanter (Children as Reliable Sources of

Information). In Jensen, M. K. (Ed.) *Interview Med Born (Interviews With Children)*. Copenhagan, National Institute of Social Research.

Titmuss, R. M. (1958) *Essays on The Welfare State*. London, George Allen and Unwin.

Tomlinson, D. and Trew, W. (2002) *Equalising Opportunities, Minimising Oppression*. London, Routledge.

TOPPS. (2000) *National Occupational Standards for Child Care at Post Qualifying Level*. London, TOPPS.

Townsend, P. (1993) *The International Analysis of Poverty*. Hemel Hempstead, Harvester Wheatsheaf.

Treacher, A. (1995) Reviewing Consumer Studies of Therapy.In Treacher A and Reimers S *Introducing User-Friendly Family Therapy*. London, Routledge.

Treseder, P. (1997) *Empowering Children and Young People: A Training Manual for Promoting Involvement in Decision-Making*. London, Save The Children.

Trevino, F. (1999) Quality of Health Care for Ethnic/Racial Minority Populations. *Ethnicity and Health*. 4: 3, 153–64.

Trevithick, P. (2000) *Social Work Skills*. Buckingham, Open University Press.

Triseliotis J. (1995) *Teenagers and The Social Work Services*. London, HMSO.

Trowell, J. and Bower, M. (1995) *The Emotional Needs of Children and Their Families*. London, Routledge.

Tucker, S., Strange, C., Cordeaux, C., Moules, T. and Torrance, N. (1999) Developing an Interdisciplinary Framework for The Education and Training of Those Working With Children and Young People. *Journal of Interprofessional Care*. 13: 3, 261–70.

Tunstill, J. (1996) Family Support: Past Present and Future Challenges. *Child and Family Social Work*. 1: 151–8.

UNICEF. (2000) *Child Poverty in Rich Nations*. New York, UNICEF, Innocenti Research Centre.

United Nations. (1989) *UN Convention on The Rights of The Child*. New York, United Nations.

Utting, D. (1995) *Family and Parenthood: Supporting Families, Preventing Breakdown*. York, Joseph Rowntree Foundation.

Vandenberg, J. and Grealish, M. (1996) Individualized Services and Supports Through the Wraparound Process: Philosophy and Procedures. *Journal of Child and Family Studies*. 5: 7–21.

Vasta, R., Haith, R. and Miller, S. (1993) *Child Psychology*. John Wiley, New York.

Vincent, J. and Jouriles, E. (Eds.) (2000) *Domestic Violence: Guidelines for Research Informed Practice*. London, Jessica Kingsley.

Vostanis, P. and Cumella, S. (1999) *Homeless Children: Problems and Needs*. London, Jessica Kingsley.

Walker, S. (1995) Family Therapy: Concepts, Models and Applications. *Nursing Times*. 91: 38, 36–7.

Walker, S. (1997) In Confidence. *Journal of Community Nursing*. 11: 7, 42–4.

Walker, S. (1999) Child Mental Health: Promoting Prevention. *Journal of Child Health Care*. 3: 4, 12–6.

Walker, S. (2001a) Developing Child and Adolescent Mental Health Services. *Journal of Child Health Care*. 5: 2, 71–6.

Walker, S. (2001b) Consulting With Children and Young People. *The International Journal of Children's Rights*. 9: 45–56.

Walker, S. (2001c) Tracing the Contours of Postmodern Social Work. *British Journal of Social Work*. 31: 29–39.

Walker, S. (2001d) Domestic Violence: Analysis of a Community Safety Alarm System. *Child Abuse Review*. 10: 170–82.

Walker, S. (2001e) Family Support and Social Work Practice: Opportunities for Child Mental Health Work. *Social Work and Social Sciences Review*. 9: 2, 25–40.

Walker, S. (2002) Family Support and Social Work Practice: Renaissance or Retrenchment? *European Journal of Social Work*. 5: 1, 43–54.

Wallace, S., Crown, J., Cox, A. and Berger, M. (1995) *Epidemiologically Based Needs Assessment: Child and Adolescent Mental Health*. Wessex Institute of Public Health.

Watkins, D. and Gerong, A. (1997) Culture and Spontaneous Self-Concepts Among Filipino College Students. *Journal of Social Psychology*. 137: 480–8.

Weaver, H. and Burns, B. (2001) I Shout With Fear at Night: Understanding the Traumatic Experiences of Refugee and Asylum Seekers. *Journal of Social Work*. 1: 2, 147–64.

Webster-Stratton, C. (1997) Treating Children With Early-onset Conduct Problems: A Comparison of Child and Parent Training Interventions. *Journal of Consulting and Clinical Psychology*. 65: 1, 93–109.

White, K. (Ed.) (1999) *Children and Social Exclusion*. London, NCVCCO.

WHO. (1992) *International Classification of Diseases (ICD 10)*. New York. WHO.

WHO. (2001) *World Health Day. Mental Health: Stop Exclusion-Dare to Care*. Geneva, WHO.

Williams, B., Catell, D., Greenwood, M., Lefevre, S., Murray, I. and Thomas, P. (1999) Exploring Person Centredness: User Perspectives on a Model of Social Psychiatry. *Health and Social Care in the Community*. 7: 6, 475–82.

Williamson, H. and Butler, I. (1996) No One Ever Listens to Us. In Cloke, C. and Davies, M. (Eds.) *Participation and Empowerment in Child Protection*. Pitman, London.

Wilson, J. (1999) *Child Focused Practice*. London, Karnac Books.

Winkley, L. (1996) *Emotional Problems in Children and Young People*. London, Cassell.

Woodhead, M. (1997) Psychology and The Cultural Construction of Children's Needs. In James, A. and Prout, A. (Eds.) *Constructing and Reconstructing Childhood*. London, Falmer Press.

Woodhead, M. (1998) Understanding Child Development in The Context of Children's Rights. In Cunninghame, C. (Ed.) *Realising Children's Rights*. London, Save The Children.

Woods, M. and Hollis, F. (1990) *Casework: A Psychological Process*. (2nd edn.) New York, Random House.

Yelloly, M. (1980) *Social Work Theory and Psychoanalysis*. New York, Van Nostrand.

Young, K. and Haynes, R. (1993) Assessing Population Needs in Primary Health Care: The Problem of GOP Attachments. *Journal of Interprofessional Care*. 7: 1, 15–27.

Young, M. and Wilmott, P. (1957) *Family and Kinship in East London*. London, Routledge Kegan, Paul.

Young Minds. (2001) *Briefing on The NSF for Mental Health*. London, Young Minds.

Youth Justice Board. (2002) *Building on Success: YJB Annual Review*. London, HMSO.